The Irish Countryman

CONRAD M. ARENSBERG received his A.B. and Ph.D. degrees in anthropology from Harvard University. He has taught at the Massachusetts Institute of Technology, Brooklyn College, Barnard College, and is currently Professor of Anthropology at Columbia University.

A distinguished scholar, Dr. Arensberg has also written numerous articles and several books including *Introducing Social Change* with Arthur H. Niehoff, and *Culture and Community* and *Family and Community in Ireland* with S. T. Kimball.

THE IRISH
COUNTRYMAN

An Anthropological Study

❦

CONRAD M. ARENSBERG

AMERICAN MUSEUM SCIENCE BOOKS

Published for
The American Museum of Natural History

The Natural History Press
Garden City, New York

The Irish Countryman was originally published by The Mac-
millan Company in 1937. The American Museum Science
Books edition is published by arrangement with Conrad
M. Arensberg.

AMERICAN MUSEUM SCIENCE BOOKS EDITION: 1968

Library of Congress Catalog Card Number 68–13630
Preface Copyright © 1968 by Conrad M. Arensberg
Printed in the United States of America

Preface

It is a pleasure to be asked, on the occasion of the reissue of this little book, to think back to a time and a place, thirty years past, yet still alive in every memory. The book is slenderer now. There have been many other anthropological studies of countries of complex civilization and ancient tradition, most of them fuller and more informed about their host countries than this one ever was. There are fuller studies of Irish culture done since or about to appear. The author is stouter, if only in the weight of intervening years of teaching, watching, and working in the growth of social science. But the country and the tradition of Ireland are with us, still deeper and richer, though now ever more modernized. May God keep them so, "go bragh." The generation of Irish country people and of townsfolk who helped the young man of thirty years ago learn something of their country and their ways is going or gone, as is the young man himself. But the memory of their kindnesses, their wit, and their wisdom is still green. That the book perhaps caught some of these qualities of theirs may account for the fact that it is, it seems, still read. I am happy to be told that people still turn to it, both for its analysis of a culture as a way of life, and for its interpretation, right or wrong, of Ireland.

The book was a modest member of a company of pioneers in 1937. The Lynds had written *Middletown*,

Lloyd Warner and his collaborators had worked *Yankee City* and were also in *Deep South* and the Middle West *Jonesville,* in the U.S.A.; Robert Redfield and Horace Miner were doing anthropological community studies in Mexico and in Canada, respectively; but this book and its successor, done with my colleague Solon Kimball, *Family and Community in Ireland* (Cambridge, Massachusetts, Harvard University Press, 1940), were the first of the cultural-anthropological studies, now so widely distributed, to cross the ocean to the Old World of Europe and high civilization. Just recently (1966) Ronald Frankenberg, from Manchester University, has published a scholarly résumé and generalization of ten subsequent social-anthropological studies done in the British Isles alone. Community studies, treating the custom and the social behavior of ways of life both rural and urban, both traditional and modern, have become one of the prime sources of social science data and discovery. Modern social anthropology and sociology draw on them from nearly every modern and developing country, from every continent.

Frankenberg's book, *Communities in Britain: Social Life in Town and Country* (London, Penguin Books, 1966), starts with our study of County Clare, and he goes quickly on to show his readers the richer and richer veins of sociological fact, insight, and conceptual understanding that modern study of contemporary living in town, country, and city have uncovered in the five countries of the British Isles. Kimball and I, likewise, but more broadly, have also recently tried to summarize the experience of social science in community studies everywhere, in Europe, Asia, America, Africa (indeed, round the world), and to show their rich contribution to modern sociology and anthropology and their illumination of the way of life and the

currents of cultural change extant in human kind in
the twentieth century (*Culture and Community*,
Conrad M. Arensberg and Solon T. Kimball, Harcourt,
Brace & World). The small group of pioneer efforts
to use anthropological analysis on the customs, traditions, and realities of modern nations, of which *The
Irish Countryman*, as you will see, was one, has grown
into a rich literature.

There are newer analyses of Irish custom, too. But
they do not yet make, unfortunately, any vast literature. Some are historical and literary, of course, but
a few are sociological and anthropological, too. For
the first category, Frank O'Connor and Sean O'Faolain
should be your literary guides and the incomparable
The Irish Heritage of Estyn Evans, your historical one.
For the second category, the good new fare is just beginning to appear. Father Alexander Humphreys's
magisterial book, *The New Dubliners* (London,
Routledge & Kegan Paul, 1966), follows our countrymen into the city and a new generation. Robert Cres-
well, from France, and Art Gallaher, from Kentucky,
have done community studies, checking up on me and
Kimball ("replication" it is called by scientists),
among small farmers of Galway and Clare. Both au-
thors' studies are soon to appear, and along with much
current Irish periodical writing they will have much
to say of the new conditions which have succeeded
those I reported in *The Irish Countryman*. It is of es-
pecial interest, of course, that since I wrote indus-
trialization has grown apace, some slacking off of emigration is at long last keeping a greater number of
young people at home, and while late marriage seems
still to prevail,[1] many country girls, it is now said,

[1] There's a book on that subject, too: *The Vanishing Irish*, ed.
John A. O'Brien, McGraw-Hill, 1953.

won't marry into farms at all; even small farm agriculture, the center of the book's concern, still flourishes, even modernizes here and there. Yet Ireland is still Irish, never fear.

These newer analyses, like the newer books, can and do give great detail, a greater richness of the discovery and the interpretation of ethnographic *minutiae*, of sociological and economic forces, of psychological stresses, resolutions, and trends in Irish life and society. The science has grown much in its command of these things, and many more persons have come to write about the people and the country than before, as recognition of their distinctiveness and of their contribution in and to our common civilization has matured. In these regards the book is always much too thin.

But I can hope, nonetheless, that the book still serves a purpose. It can still offer an introduction to Irish life and to Irish rural custom and to the interwoven causes and effects explaining the cultural system, the work, the family life, the loyalties, and the values connecting them. The book still makes its scientific point of functionalism, of the perception of system in the explanation of human social life. I can hope also that the book may still evoke, as it seems to have done, much nostalgia and much recognition from Irish persons (the Gaels, at home and beyond the seas), and much affectionate and sympathetic curiosity, as it seems also to have done, from the non-Irish lovers of and visitors to their country and tradition (the Gall, as the old language used to separate them). That is as it should be, because anthropology, the science of human beings, can never be only objective, like cold metallurgy. It must also teach us humanity, an empathy for the range and the variety of human beings, at home and round the world.

C.M.A.

COLUMBIA UNIVERSITY
NEW YORK, N.Y.
1968

Preface

It is a rash undertaking for any man, however ripe in experience he may be, to attempt the interpretation of a nation's folk. When the nation he essays is not his own, and his experience is really but very little, rashness becomes foolhardiness. Yet when Dr. Lowell, president-emeritus of Harvard University, did me the honour of asking me to deliver a course of lectures at the Lowell Institute in Boston, in March 1936, I found myself impelled to take my courage in my hands. The book which follows represents the lectures given at the Institute. It is an attempt to present to the public some measure of the interest in human social behaviour and the absorbing problems of human societies which inspires and rewards the anthropologist and sociologist in his long quests in field and library. As my own quest had taken me on a definite, concrete mission to southern Ireland, I felt I should best serve my purpose by devoting myself to that country, which had so richly rewarded my own interest.

Consequently, if in these pages I make yet another contribution to the growing literature of commentary upon the Irish scene, I do so with a deep sense of humility and gratitude. My debts are perhaps greater than I realize. As an inquisitive, even importunate, stranger in a foreign land, seeking out intimacies and sanctities scarcely acknowledged among friends and fellow-countrymen, I was utterly dependent upon the hospitable good-nature and the intelligent understanding of the people among whom I worked. I never knew it to fail. My first debt is to the people of Ireland, of all walks of life, who took me in. They are too numerous to mention by name, even those whom I might well single out for special recognition. Yet if I owe any group of them a greater debt than another, it is the people of the 'Banner' County of Clare, among whom I lived.

Academic indebtedness is of a different nature. The fraternity of science is a reality today in which every practitioner has a part. One is greatly dependent upon the inspiration, the co-operation, and the criticism that fraternity affords. My own dependence has rested chiefly upon my colleagues, Professor Lloyd Warner of Chicago and Dr. Solon Kimball of Harvard, with whom I did much of the field work whose results this book records. Some of the observations made are theirs, though the responsibility for error and misjudgment is entirely my own.

But my reliance upon the aid and criticism of Professors Hooton, Tozzer and L. J. Henderson and Dr. Eliot D. Chapple, all of Harvard, has been no less great. Each in his way has contributed to the development of the interest out of which this book springs. In Ireland, too, there were other contributors, from whom much of whatever understanding of Ireland I may have derives. Professors Eoin MacNeil and George O'Brien of the National University, Drs. Henry Kennedy and Seumas O Duilearga of Dublin and Daniel Coghlan of Ennis all led me along their chosen paths. Through the friendship and encouragement of Mr. Patrick Meghen of the Irish Civil Service many a door to Irish life fell open. In dedicating the book to him and to Professor Warner I make what little recognition of their parts in it I can.

C.M.A.

HARVARD UNIVERSITY
CAMBRIDGE, MASS.
SEPTEMBER 1936

Contents

		PAGE
I	The Interpretation of Custom	21
II	Countrymen at Work	48
III	The Family and the Land	76
IV	Boys and Men	105
V	Shops, Pubs, and Fairs	136
VI	The Good People	163
	Index	193

I

The Interpretation of Custom

The arrival of a stranger in a west country Irish town is still an event. The age of machinery has not yet destroyed the leisure of curiosity. But when the stranger shows no intent of hurrying on, like an ordinary tourist, and sports none of the weapons of field and stream, the matter assumes no mean local importance. A new bank clerk or land commissioner is expectable; he soon sinks into the colour of his position and surroundings. Even a 'returned Yank', once his parentage and probable savings have been determined, and his clothes and manners scrutinized, soon drops out of mind.

But there is no understanding a stranger whose only apparent business is to chat with people and to walk about with notebook in hand. And when he calls himself an 'anthropologist', the mystery thickens. The 'squinting windows', for which Brinsley MacNamara once named a novel of the Irish countryside, do not soon lose their squint; and an eddy of whispered speculation follows the stranger up and down the narrow old-world streets of the town.

But time brings acceptance of most mysteries. It finds a formula for them that gives them a familiar ring. So, the anthropologist gradually found acceptance. Even his formidable title grew easier as its translation spread. The Irish today are a very literate people. And a sudden increase in the circulation of books on anthropology from the county library helped very quickly to establish the anthropologist as 'looking for old customs'.

Once, perhaps, the translation would have been adequate. But anthropology today is much more than a search for ancient custom. Even in Ireland, where the traditional Celtic life still lingers on, the anthropologist must conceive his purpose in broader terms. I want to devote this first lecture to the new purpose and its application to the Irish scene. In the remaining five lectures I shall try to present to you certain of the factors of custom and belief in the countryside of the south and west of Ireland and to analyse them in terms of the purpose we discuss here.

First of all we must clear up the matter of presumption. It may seem presumptuous that an anthropologist should profess to discuss the life of a modern nation. To some of us it may seem something like an engineer or a physicist, who deserts his field for metaphysics and morals. To others it may seem to betray a rather derogatory attitude toward the nation discussed. But neither desertion nor derogation can rightfully be charged. Our confusion, if we do have it, springs from our associations with the word 'anthropology'.

We are prone to think of the anthropologist as a collector of strange facts about savage, and at best, semi-civilized peoples. When analogues to these facts appear from time to time among civilized men we regard them as superstitious survivals at best, worthy of our study only as *curiosa*. Why then an anthropology of modern Ireland? Whatever we may think of her, we cannot include Ireland among the primitive and barbarous peoples. If we go on to relate primitive survivals to the way of life of the Irish country-people, we certainly do not condemn them wholesale as bar-

barians, nor can we rightfully regard them as primitive.

If this is the case, our associations with the word 'anthropology' must be at fault. So let us set about revising them.

To make the revision is really to explain the development of anthropological science. In common with the rest of us, the anthropologists have gone through something of a mental and moral revolution. The changes in the conceptual basis of science, rapidly spreading in the last thirty years, have not passed them by.

Long ago it was necessary to give up all hope of establishing unilinear evolution. The student of man had very early to admit that the course of humanity's growth was no simple straight path. At first he had thought of the primitive as a backward child, held back in the lower grades of mankind's school of experience. That view broke down. With new evidence it became clear that there were many schools. To continue the figure, it grew apparent that the schools were only indirectly comparable and that they had very little of common curriculum. Each people makes its own adaptation. Today it is these adaptations rather than historical continuities which invite comparison.

The very evidence that had led us to believe in a common curriculum began to take on a new meaning. All modern societies, our own included, present many continuities with supposed prior states of human development. The evolutionary analogy gives us their name—they are survivals: earmarks of a lower and outmoded way of life. In the analogy of the child, they are obscure memories of forgotten childhood.

But today the analogy of the child falls down too. The psycho-analyst finds the mind of childhood by no means forgotten in the adult. His work has stripped the adult of his mask of rationality and laid bare the subconscious unreason below. Much the same development took place in anthropology. The field ethnologist soon demolished civilized man's pretension to the sole possession of the adult mind. One cannot read a page of modern ethnological description from Malinowski in Melanesia to the Herskovitses in Guiana without a shock to one's complacency. The savage mixes the rational and irrational in much the same way as we do. Only the ingredients of the mixture are different. The work of a Pareto on our own society helps to tear away the last threads of our illusion. For he could devote four great volumes to our non-logicality!

Along with this new realization the anthropologist was forced to share the moral uncertainties of our age. We are no longer so sure of progress as our fathers and grandfathers were. Nor are we so sure that today our civilization is the highest point yet reached in man's upward sweep to an inevitable perfection. Relativity has invaded even our valuation of civilization.

But this shaking of our convictions has not been without one good result, at least in the science of man. It has led to an ever greater objectivity. It has enabled us to see moral absolutes themselves as expressions of particular times and places. The anthropologist had to learn this tolerance very early. To carry his own valuation into a thousand different moral atmospheres over the world was to invite a thousand antagonisms and to learn nothing, except perhaps invective. 'Customs beastly, manners none', was great invective but it added little to our knowledge.

It is the search for new facts that has brought a new face upon anthropology. Non-normative science is the statement of relationship between observed data. But the reconstructions of human history to which evolutionary ideas had led cannot be observed. On the other hand, the actualities of primitive life in the present lie before one's eyes. New facts were still at hand if one hurried to look for them.

As the result, field work gained immensely in value and prestige. It was not enough to discuss a particular trait or custom, to follow its temporal and spatial course, to trace it from time to time and tribe to tribe. This was a valuable inquiry, but it led nowhere beyond its avowed purpose: a study of cultural diffusion and human interchange. It could not even be, as it hoped, a record of human inventiveness, for the origin of culture traits is lost in the mists of the past.

The limitations, then, of the diffusionist technique forced attention in a new direction. Detailed study of the particular field began to command interest. The tribe, the savage community, the clan, might throw into relief new facts. The focus of interest need no longer be the culture-trait nor the single custom, better perhaps to look at the human beings who are the momentary bearers of the culture. It is paradoxical that the science of man should stand in need of a thorough humanizing. But it did, and a long course of ethnological work was necessary to bring it about.

The new facts were human rather than cultural data. This does not sound so revolutionary. The anthropologist has always written about man's doings and sought to explain them. But he had never made them the central focus of his interest in savages and primitives. It was in this shift of emphasis that the revolution lay.

To give crude examples, the change was of this sort. Once the question asked was whether this or that tribe practised monogamy and from whom it acquired the habit; what was the development of monogamy and what prior states did it succeed. Now the question became rather, "What do the tribesmen do and think in getting mates, what makes them act so, and how do their actions affect other departments of their lives?" Where once a savage who used the bow was asked, "Where did you get it, and how did you learn to make your particular kind of bow?" Now he was asked, "What use do you make of your bow, what does it mean to you and your friends, with whom do you share its quarry, and why do you flourish it so in your dances?"

In other words, it was a shift from a history of forms and institutions to a study of behaviour. The answers to the new questions might not illuminate us about human evolutions, but they would not be any the less valuable as data of human behaviour.

As you can see, this new curiosity was social. Man is a social creature. The study of his customs is a study of social behaviour, for he acts as a member of a family, clan, tribe, or community. It early became very clear that his customs had an intimate relation to the life of his groups; their meaning lay in the social adaptation of the individual.

Once this step had been taken anthropology had to recognize its new face. It must conceive itself more and more as a social science.

Thus the term 'social anthropology', an old term, underwent a shift in meaning. It came to cover the field that it occupies in this discussion. The branch of the study of man which deals as we are going to do, with his acts rather than his anatomy or physiognomy or the archaeological remains of his past cultures, had gone through a revolution which brought it next door to a sociology.

But the social branch of anthropology reached the study of man as a social creature through a different course from that followed by more conventional sociologies. It came to the social field with its own techniques and its own experience.

Consequently, it felt it could make a contribution of its own. The barrier between the barbarian and the civilized man, as we have seen, is no longer conceivable in simple terms. Typically modern logic is not at all a *rara avis* among Bushmen; typically 'primitive' behaviour characterizes us all at moments. We even share many institutions with our savage brothers (or third cousins, if you prefer)—such as the family, the association, even political forms such as royalty and the democratic vote (an Iroquois habit). We like to think of these as 'rudimentary forms', it is true. But that salves our pride without removing the fact of our likeness to the primitive.

The anthropologist's experience in such matters, he felt, was of particular importance. He had been led to it in his study of primitive communities. There he was brought face to face with social wholes. He caught a glimpse of the forest beyond the separate trees. He could see his people whole, above and beyond the discrete parts of their culture—institutions, particularities of custom, categories of belief. This was the experience he felt made him eligible for trying his hand in a larger field.

He gained this confidence, as I have said, as a direct result of a new emphasis upon human behaviour—part of the humanizing of the savage I have mentioned. The new emphasis soon developed into a study of wholes. Most primitive peoples are small in number. Yet even so they exhibit all the characteristics of a large society. They are minuscule social systems. The activities we name economics, literature, art, philosophy, religion, manners, pedagogy, law, custom, government, are all present among them. Only the words for them are lacking; and their differentiation is less marked.

For the observer the difference in scale has an immense value. It allows him an objective view of the whole which is practically impossible in our own modern life. It throws the articulation of the parts into relief. Half of his work of isolating relationships is done for him already, by the very simplicity the scale demands.

The value of the smaller scale does not stop there. In sociology today, the immensity of our society and the infinity of kinds of behaviour which it entails makes the clearing away of obscuring data and the definition of manageable social problems a colossal task. Think what it means to study, let us say, politics, not for political theory but for political practice. Or what it means to portray the political party not for what it is or ought to be, but for its function in the multiple lives which it affects. A Lincoln Steffens might do it after a life of muckraking, an Al Smith might do it were he more articulate. But how little even their wide experience can help us along the road to formulating generalities capable of explaining the real behaviour of individuals in the realm we label politics! Difficult as such a task is, it pales into a sinecure before the further task of interpreting, say, a Tammany Hall, not as a blot upon the fair face of American civic life, but in its relation to laws governing the behaviour of mankind.

I do not for a moment suggest that the social anthropologist at work among primitives has found the open sesame to such immensities as these. But I do hope to show that he has a first clue. I hope I can demonstrate to you that the smaller scale in which he could work upon comparable problems in minute social systems affords a technique which has a bearing on such queries.

For when in the Trobriands of Melanesia a dispute among brothers can arise out of and set in motion the whole traditional, habitual apparatus of tribal life—when the means of settlement adopted reveal the patterns of social action which make up the reciprocities binding tribesman to tribesman and kinsman to kinsman—when magic and spirit-lore can be seen at work influencing the conduct of this and that member of the community in such a way as to canalize the retribution the offender comes to make—when in fact, all of the patterns of tribal life are swung into action round a nuclear disturbance in conventional behaviour, as in the case of the suicide who assuaged his crime of clan-incest, then the dynamic functions of a whole social system are capable of description. The smallness of the scale, and the complete detachment of the ethnologist, affords a chance for an objective analysis of social forces as controllable and as demonstrable as a study of chemical interaction.

This experience of dynamic social wholes growing out of individual behaviour steels the anthropologist to make the step into modern life. Those who have read the Lynds on 'Middletown' can remember the pioneer attempt. It was a formal field research, largely descriptive. With the Lynds, not even Main Street is safe from the ethnologist's prying eye. Since then, other studies more and more analytical in character have begun and are progressing. If Main Street has become fair game for the anthropologist, Ireland has little to fear.

I am afraid I have been very long in getting back to Ireland and the 'collector of old customs'. I hope you have borne with me. You can see now how inadequate the countryside's translation was. Old custom and belief *are* our concern, but our *emphasis* is a new one. What do the old customs alive today mean for the countryman? What is the way of life of which they are still a part after centuries of existence? It is all very well to speculate about their origin in the dim mist of time; we shall do some of that. But we shall not rely on that speculation entirely. If we do so, we forgo the opportunity the present gives us.

The present can tell one little enough of what a given custom or belief meant at its inception. But it *can* teach one what it means now, in the lives of the persons who follow the custom or hold the belief.

But care must be taken not to make this new inquiry a matter of speculation. Interpretation should be put to the test of experience. Anthropology, in one of its many branches, has grown from a history largely conjectural to a social dynamics. It has become a behavioural, or better, an operational science, to use the term Bridgman has introduced into the natural sciences. If the anthropologist avoids all explanations except those which arise out of his observations of what men do, and if he accepts them only when he can test them again against observed behaviour, he will be, if only imperfectly, in the main line of scientific development.

Before one makes a frontal attack, it is good tactics to survey one's ground. One likes to know what interest it holds in store.

Ireland, particularly Celtic southern Ireland, has always had a fascination for most of us. The cities, particularly Dublin, the last stronghold of the art of conversation, are as charming as the countryside. But it is the country districts which occupy us here.

Most of us probably know at least four countrysides

in Ireland. Like Caesar we divide our Gaul. But the divisions we make are not geographical. Our four Irelands are lands of the spirit.

Perhaps our first Ireland is the mystic land of the past. This is the land of the 'Celtic twilight', the country of Synge and Yeats and Stephens. It is the seat of an age-old tradition, of the remains of a once brilliant Celtic civilization. Literature has taught us to look for this land in the barren moors and rugged mountains of the west, among the tiny white cabins of Connemara and along the misty headlands of Kerry and West Cork. It is the Ireland of Aran and the Blaskets. There a remnant of the sagas and hero-tales can still be heard, a wandering poet sang but yesterday in the lilt of Blind Raferty. There old men and old women sitting by turf fires still spin tales of banshees and the good people; and just the other day in Daniel Corkery's hidden Munster the hedge school-master and the wandering scholar had Ovid and Horace at his tongue's tip. And there too the riders to the sea go down to their deaths amid the keening women, whose language rings to us of simple, old-world poetry long ago passed from our own tongues.

A second Ireland is a gay, full-blooded picture, though some among the nationalists dislike it. It is the Ireland of the merry and happy-go-lucky present. Handled badly, it becomes the land of the 'stage-Irishman', that buffoonish figure which the nation's pride so justly resents. But handled well, by a Lady Gregory, a George Birmingham, and on the stage by the Abbey Players, it is a world of its own. In it, innocent boasting, the excitement of a race-meeting, the hurly-burly of a fair, the flashing wit of a court-room, and the staccato thunder of a political campaign, reveal a talkative, mercurial, witty people, amusing and intelligent, romantic and gallant.

The third Ireland most of us know is a more serious scene. One might even call it a grimmer land. It is a sober, hard-working land of minute towns and small farms upon a soil not always grateful. It is a land of hard realities. This Ireland is subject to hot flashes of anger and dispute which throw into relief deep-lying hatreds and fierce loyalties. We all know something of the Land War and Sinn Fein and the bitter internecine strife of the Trouble. If we know anything of Ireland's history we see these rough upheavals of a tranquil scene as great punctuation marks upon a red page of struggle lasting seven hundred years. This is the Ireland of bitter economic fate and political unrest. Much of this can be laid at England's door, but not all. The Ireland of the Irish is no more free of internal strife than any other land.

Most of us recognize a fourth Ireland as well, especially those who are Catholics. It is the Ireland of the Faith, the Island of Saints and Scholars. It is the land of the devout, where word and deed breathe a religious fervour which most of us have forgotten. This is the land of holy wells and pilgrimages and roadside shrines. Well-filled churches rise above every hamlet now and the black-frocked priest is a familiar friendly figure. To many of us, perhaps a paradox lies here. Fierce love of political liberty goes hand in hand with a deep devotion to the most authoritarian of Christian creeds.

Nor is this the only paradox in a land of surprises where even the sun and sky are inconsistent. The beauty of the Irish landscape lies in the never-ending change of colour. A momentary break of sun transforms the sky from dull yellow to bright, rain-washed blue. It lights a hillside to brilliant green, or mottles it in brown and green and mauve. A moment later it disappears, dashing the sky back again to mournful purples and misty greys. So it is with the Irish character. What is too harshly called the 'superstition' of Irish folklore coexists with Catholic piety; a puritanical morality goes hand in hand with the hilarity of a race-meeting. The loyalty too harshly named 'clannishness' runs side by side with the personal acquisitiveness of a peasant proprietorship. Small wonder then the Irish feel no foreigner will ever fully understand.

This is the terrain in which I hope to campaign. If we are to make an attempt at a whole view, we must see the country whole. I must try to show you all four Irelands.

For the inhabitants of this fourfold land are 'Irishmen All', as George Birmingham once named a book. But unlike his characters they are all the same people. The inhabitants of the countryside dwell in all four of our lands of the spirit. The division we make is only illusive. It marks our interests, not the realities of the Irishman's life.

That life, so various, so capable of being looked at from many angles, affords many fascinating questions to us in pursuance of our study. What are its laws? How does it relate to old custom and belief?

This people preserves an unbroken ancient tradition that goes back, perhaps long into pre-Christian times. Their variant of Celtic culture and language is lost in prehistory. Yet isolation here in the 'outpost of western Europe' has preserved it. Today the historian is in a better position to understand the history of all Europe because the Celtic past has survived latest here, outliving Roman and Christian inundation only here.

For that reason, and because it is still a comparatively unknown province archaeologically, Ireland has become a favourite ground for many others of the students of man who stand under the umbrella of an-

thropology. The folklorist has discovered Ireland, and
today the Free State Government subsidizes the preservation of folklore as a monument to national great-
ness. The ethnographer finds primitive tools and
house-forms, even a wooden plough of Bronze-age
days, still in use in remote Waterford or Connemara
mountains. The archaeologist 'roots up the raths and
the forts', as the country-people say, and lays bare the
prehistoric life.

Harvard has played and is still playing a great part
in the discovery of Ireland's past. To date four expe-
ditions have gone out. Under the ultimate direction
of Dr. Hooton of Harvard they have excavated widely
in various parts of the country. The findings of Dr.
Hugh Hencken and Mr. Hallam Movius have opened
up a new chapter in our knowledge of European prehistory and in the history of Celtic culture. It is too
early to give a full summary of these discoveries, and,
of course, the privilege should be reserved for the dis-
coverers. But we can say that much of the darkness
of Bronze- and early Iron-age Ireland is lifting. The
matter is of interest to us here because it pushes backward the continuities whose final stages will come up
in our discussion of the present rural culture.

A people whose life, at least in some of its aspects,
has so ancient and so unbroken an historical continuity
could not fail to excite the interest of still another
kind of anthropologist. In one aspect, the study of
man is a human zoology. Man, like all animals, has his
species, his subspecies, his races, and his hereditary
strains. These differ in physical traits, in morphologi-
cal characters, and, perhaps, in inherent propensities
and abilities. The reduction of man's physical and
hereditary variations to uniform laws is a legitimate
pursuit in science and one of great interest and importance to us all. Harvard has taken a lead in this

field, physical anthropology, in Ireland in recent years. Again under Dr. Hooton's direction, Mr. Wesly Dupertuis has undertaken the physical measurement of large samples of the Irish people throughout the country. The result will be a knowledge of Irish physical type comparable, or even superior, to that we possess of other European peoples. Some day we may know more certainly the biologically determined inherencies of man. Then perhaps our knowledge of the strains which make up the peoples of the world, Ireland included, may stand us in good stead.

Already such work as this will show us the relation of the Irish to other European strains and help us to trace out historical currents in the country. Think of the field such work opens! Where is the Gael pure today? Who is the Firbolg, the aboriginal whom the Milesians found in possession? Who and where are the invading Gall? Briton, Norman, Dane, Fleming, Saxon, Englishman and Scotsman brought their bloods to this land and mingled them with the Gael. What traces have they all left and what bloods are at work today?

All these queries, nevertheless, do not primarily concern us in this discussion. The antiquity of some of the data stimulates another inquiry. But we cannot escape the sway of these other considerations entirely. There is no reason why we should. Even if they can offer us no direct aid, they can, nevertheless, afford us a stimulation.

Some such thoughts as these must have been in the social anthropologist's mind when he first made his way into a rural community. I cannot speak for my colleagues, Mr. Warner of Chicago University and Mr. Kimball of Harvard, who helped to gather the field material on Ireland. But I *can* speak for myself.

I felt Ireland's fascination as I toiled along behind

my bicycle up the mountain road that runs from the
narrow valley lands at <u>Doolin</u> in the extreme northwest of <u>County Clare.</u> I was on my way to my first
stay in an Irish west-country farm community. My
road, no wider than a bridle-path, led up a sharp es-
carpment out of the tiny valley which empties its stony
river into the Atlantic, not three miles away from the
southernmost island of Aran. Once the top of the rim
is reached the mountainside flattens out into a green
and gently sloping table-land. Standing there one can
see the whaleback rocks that are the Aran Islands and
the masses of Mount Elva on the southern shore of
Galway Bay. Far beyond in Connemara, one can catch
the glint of the Twelve Pins, if the day is 'hard' and
sunny. Off to the left, the table-land breaks off
abruptly three hundred feet downward into the Atlantic, for the famed Cliffs of Moher are here, reminders of an Irish mountain that the sea has shorn off
clean.

The community toward which I was making my
way lies along the table-land between mountaintop of
bracken and black bog and the cliffs. It keeps up the
old tradition. It calls itself Luogh, and its language,
at least that of the old people, is Irish, but the young
people are forgetting the old tongue. English is the
more common speech today, even here. Yet Mr. Delargy, the editor of the *Irish Folklore Journal*, has collected a large number of stories, songs and traditional
tales and sayings here, some of them going back to the
saga cycles.

Luogh is remote. It is nearly half a day's tramp
along the roads from its market town, Ennistymon.
Even Ennistymon is no metropolis. It is a sprawling
village of 1200 people. Neither bus nor train runs between the two.

But Luogh is not entirely isolated by this remoteness. It does not entirely escape modernity. Pleasure-bent motorists from the cities drive through along the cliffs. One can see Atlantic liners standing-to just outside Galway Bay. Many of Luogh's farms have a horse-drawn mowing machine, out of an English steel works, and some of the houses own a mechanical cream separator, even though next door a wooden hand churn is still in use which looks no different from those found deep in the bogs.

But modern tools do not make the life of Luogh. They ease it perhaps, and work a slow effect. But in a short stay one cannot see that change. One's attention turns to the life into which these few strays of modernity find their way.

For Luogh is like many another community of small farms over Clare and southern and western Ireland. Some lie closer to urban centres, some are even more remote. Many are better off; some few are poorer. Some have kept the Irish language better; others have abandoned it altogether for the brogue. But they all have the 'sweet *blas*' of Gaelic still on their tongues and speak an idiom embedded in their common folk life.

I did not know this as I came to Luogh. But I was to learn it soon in Luogh and in other communities in County Clare. Later I was to find it so even more widely; in newspapers, in novels, in court records, in statistical reports, in political bombasts. It was a way of life with its own laws which included Luogh and the Blaskets and even the fertile small farms of rich Tipperary.

When I first came to Luogh I knew only that in this remote little community of small farmers I should find something of the old tradition still alive. My learning was a piecemeal process—a sketching out of wider and

wider ramifications of the observations which came
my way.

It is this process to which I wish to devote the re-
mainder of this lecture. It is a process in which you
can follow me. Perhaps better than anything else it
will prepare us for an anthropological study of Irish
rural life.

Let me illustrate this process with two examples. I
shall call them the 'west room' and the 'old man's
curse'. Both of them are related to old custom and
both will serve to show the process by which one lays
bare the rural life of which old custom is a part.

The house to which my road into Luogh finally led
was a typical small farmer's cottage. It was one of
twenty-six in Luogh. It was the seat of a small farm
of sixteen acres (with eight more in the valley), 'the
place of four cows and a horse', as the country-people
describe it. Much of it was rough, wet mountain land,
but the phrase implies that it was good enough at least
to provide grass for animals. All farms are described
in this way, for by the cows and the small 'gardens'
of potatoes, cabbage, oats and turnips, the small farmers live. We shall have more to say of agriculture in
another context; I think the explanation is sufficient
here.

My host's house in Luogh, as I have said, was like
the others. It was a bit 'stronger', that is, neater, better
built and kept, than many of the others, but it was
like the others in all essentials. It was a white-washed
stone cottage, rectangular, roofed with slate (though
it was only a few years ago that they gave up thatch).
Its long sides faced roughly north and south, each with
a door opening directly out into the yards. In the gable
of the roof was a loft for sleeping; otherwise it was
confined to a single story. The central room, the largest by far, was the kitchen. There the family passed

their lives and prepared and ate the food cooked on the hearth. The hearth was an open turf fire, built in a chimney large enough to have two hobs or seats deep within on either side. It had, too, an iron hook which swung the cooking-pots out into the room from off the fire.

Behind this hearth was another room. It was called, for its position in the house, the 'west room'. This is the west room which is to provide my first example.

In most countrymen's houses, especially in poorer regions, the west room, that behind the hearth, is the only room except for the kitchen and the loft. In some houses, however, there is another room too. This is usually a bedroom, at the opposite end of the kitchen. This was the case at my host's.

But in either case it soon becomes apparent that there is something special about the west room. At Luogh this struck one's eye immediately. At my host's the room was a sort of parlour into which none but distinguished guests were admitted. In it were kept pictures of the dead and emigrated members of the family, all 'fine' pieces of furniture, symbolic brass objects brought in by the bride at marriage; the sacramentals used when mass was celebrated in the house, in fact all religious objects, crucifixes, and so forth, except the 'blessed lamp' and a 'holy picture' in the kitchen. Nor were my hosts alone in keeping objects of sentimental and religious value in this special room. Other houses did likewise. The general feeling was that such objects 'belonged' there.

But these facts had little significance until others began to appear. Here we enter the realm which we ordinarily call 'old custom'. The west room had still another association, of a supernatural cast. This appeared only gradually. The west room was of central importance in fairy-lore.

In this all Luogh concurred, though few could be found to give it expression. The cult of the fairies, these days, is branded as 'superstition'. It is under fire from townsman, school-teacher, and priest. But even those who could express no views could be seen to act as if they too were believers.

(Where fairy paths were remembered to pass the house, they went by the west room. Where food and water was left out at night, it was left there. No outhouse, shed, or other building could be built on this side of the house. That would bring bad luck. Very few could or would tell why; they left it to a common inference. The building would be 'in the way'. Nevertheless, reluctant as they might be to express belief, my hosts none the less practised it. No house of Luogh's twenty-six had any shed or outhouse at its western end.)

Here were two very definite associations with the west room. What did they mean? The attitudes they represented were respect, and perhaps a little fear; but it was respect that was dominant. What was this respect and why should it show itself in fairy-lore and in household furnishing?

Faced with such a problem the anthropologist's usual recourse is to history. Traditionally the west is the land of the dead. In the ancient sun-cult, in which early man has likened his own progress to that of the sun's daily and yearly course, the west is the sacred abode of the dead. Even today, we speak of dying, half jocularly, as 'going west'. In ancient Celtic mythology, the heaven at life's end, *Tír na nÓg*, and Avalon, the island of apple trees which the Greeks knew as the Garden of the Hesperides, and which in a Christian rendering the blessed Saint Brendan may have reached, lies to the west in the setting sun. It is very likely that in this folk practice there survives nearly all that remains of an elaborate early mythology.

Alas for our questioning, no one remembers Avalon in Luogh, *Tír na nÓg* is a dying legend. If you ask the old men about the west, tales of sunken cities and strange sea-creatures greet your ears; ask about the fairies and fairy paths and you get, first, indignant denials of such degrading belief, and then anecdotes, tales, incidents, which illustrate their character and their power for good and evil. Ask about the furniture of this room, and you learn only that it is the right and fitting thing that the objects fill this room and no other. No one can trace the continuity; tradition is felt in the mass rather than in the particular.

We are left then with what we can hear and observe about the present. To question upon anything else is to get nowhere; it merely starts a chain of obscuring generalities more inspired by the question than by what Luogh feels and thinks and does.

But the case is not hopeless. If one casts one's reliance upon observations and questions in the present, new facts appear. The west room figures in marriage. In the contracts drawn up it is often mentioned by name. It is the room reserved for themselves by the old people, the father and mother of the groom; they reserve it for their own use after they turn over the farm to their sons at marriage.

Ask about this and more information comes to you. It is into this room that the old couple move. The room is theirs. Younger members of the household dare not enter it except with permission. Indeed, it is the old couple who throw their aura around the room; the respect owed them is very like that felt toward the room they occupy. Here one enters a new field of behaviour and attitude in human relations. The honour and command of the old couple do not leave them altogether when they retire from active ownership of the farm. They enter a new status of which the associations round the west room are one reflexion.

So it goes, the new questions and new observations lead not to a prehistory or a chain of continuities, but to an ever-widening number of living associations which colour the relations of men and women, old and young. They lead to a realization of the laws and custom by which the small farmers find their lives ordered. In this instance, the west room of Luogh is a dim survival, perhaps, of Avalon and *Tír na nÓg*. But more certainly it is a focal point in a system of values some little of which we have begun to glimpse. Old custom in the west room thus gives us the first example of our method. An inquiry into the present of rural life leads us into the ways of human behaviour rather than into those of cultural descent.

I called my second example 'the old man's curse'. It is perhaps not so pleasant an example and it springs out of infinitely rarer occasions. Yet it will serve as well as did the west room to show us where our queries must lie. The example of the old man's curse concerns a lost eye. Many of the country-people believed that the curse was directly responsible for the loss of a young man's eye. The young man in question lived in a district not far from Luogh; and the old man who cursed him was a neighbour. This is the baldest possible statement of the occurrence, and it would suffice if we were interested merely in collecting instances of magical injury.

For the baneful effects of curses, of black magic, of the 'evil eye', are a commonplace of anthropological literature. They are common enough too in Irish folklore. Men suffer injury in some way from supernatural causes. The possessor of the evil eye can blight, maim, and kill; the priest's curse, though in this case uttered only for cause, can bring ruin upon a prosperous house; can turn an unbeliever's head upon his shoulder; strike blindness; and the shrill imprecations of old men and women, or the *rann* of a satiric poet, can bring equal harm. Supernatural injuries of this sort are as old as the Celtic sagas. The belief is spread, of course, far beyond Ireland. The Neapolitan fisherman paints his boat against the evil eye, the Balkan woman embroiders her petticoat to ward off evil and curses. The West African sorcerer knows the technique to perfection; our own Pennsylvania Dutch 'hexes' are modern practitioners. For the belief belongs to the infinite realm of magic.

If one were satisfied with the bald collector's statement, one would be content to leave the young man in such company. But by inquiring more deeply into the incident, one can look into the situation in which he suffered. If the belief can be seen at work in a situation which can be readily assessed, then it will serve better as a guide toward understanding the life in which it can still operate.

The situation has many elements. In the first place, the details of the young man's trouble are simple enough. In working a scythe round the bush-choked wall of a field, he fell in such a way as to drive a sliver of bush into his eye. We should call it, I suppose, a simple accident and pity him his bad luck.

But the small farmers among whom he lived wove another world of explanation round that eye. Gradually the tale unfolds. Perhaps the loss of the eye is a punishment. For the young man was not entirely blameless. An unvoiced suspicion had pointed his way.

For there had been a few weeks before what used to be called, in more heated days, 'an agrarian outrage'. Two old men, bachelors living alone, had been fired upon in the night. Someone had pumped gun-shot through the window of their poor cabin, high up the mountainside. As was probably intended, the shots buried themselves harmlessly in the cabin floor. But they awakened the old men, and frightened them badly.

The occurrence shocked the community. The two old men were harmless creatures; they were 'saints' in the country phrase. Who would want to injure them or drive them out?

The country-people had their suspicions; but the police could get nothing from them. There was nothing for the inspector to do but report another 'agrarian intimidation'. Even if he too knew, there was nothing to do; he could prove nothing without witnesses.

The country-people kept silence for good reason, from their point of view. If their suspicions were correct, the matter was a private affair, a family squabble. It was no business of theirs.

For the old men, by the standards of rural kinship, were not entirely blameless either. They held a farm they did not work. They took none of their kinsmen in. They should long ago have given up their land. One of them should have brought a girl in, married her and raised a family. They should have passed the land on to their sons, or failing sons, they should have brought in a nephew or other boy of their kindred. Then they could have turned the farm over to the boy, when they felt themselves too old, and let him marry, in order that their kindred's name continue and grow in land.

But the old men had never had a 'taste for marrying'. They were victims themselves of a too-intense loyalty. I say victims, because their loyalty had been narrowest of all. Their old mother had lived too long in her turn. She had never decided which one should get the land and bring in a girl. Perhaps their father might have decided, had he lived, but their mother survived him by many years. Neither of them wished to leave her side and neither would leave to make room for the other. When at last the mother died, the two bachelor sons were already old; they were long past marrying and set in celibate ways. They lingered on in an ever narrower round.

In the community they were 'saints', as I have said; they were 'no trouble to man or beast'. Yet, from another point of view, they were not doing the 'natural' thing; they made no provisions for their kinsmen; they did not pass on the land to those to whom by country right it should go. They refused to fill their proper roles in life. No wonder, then, that their cabin was a byword for neglect and disrepair. The countrymen would tell you, in a moralizing vein, it had become so 'for lack of a woman's hand'.

But to censure them for their misspent lives was no affair of the community's. The kindred of the old men were the aggrieved parties. Their name suffered and their sons were landless and unborn; land belonging to them lay idle. So, whoever did the shooting—perhaps he had a reason for it. Suspicion might point here and there, but whatever measures the kinsmen might take to remedy their grievance concerned the kinsmen alone. Let those to whom the old men's duty lay see that they followed it. It was best to say nothing beyond one's immediate circle.

But the community could not entirely condone the shooting either. It was a bad thing, no good could come of it. To disturb the peace in such a way shook the security of them all; it gave the district 'a bad name'.

So, when a new event took place, the community found outlet for its censure. When the young man lost his eye, the community was ready for this reaffirmation of its threatened values. For the young man was one of the aggrieved kindred; he was a landless cousin's son; to him and his brothers the old men's farm should have gone. In the loss of his eye, the community felt he paid his penalty. No one knew just how it was inflicted; one does not attempt to unveil such mysteries. Their force is too great, too little controllable. Some felt the old man's curse had done it, some felt that the priest might have done it, for the old men had appealed to him. Some blamed a vague mysterious power in the bush the young man cut. Whatever it was, the fact was plain. Only a week or so after the shooting, the young man lost his eye. His crime found a sure punishment in a realm in which all could agree without running risk of retaliation at the hands of the disputing parties.

I have couched this incident in vague, unprecise language for a reason. In the realm of folk-belief outlines are not clear and concepts are not precise. No one could formulate logically this retribution which put out the young man's eye. Nevertheless all felt it. And a moralist among them could sum up: "It is right to respect the old people".

The second example, then, points in the same direction as the first. Both west room and the old man's curse reflect age-old tradition. But both reveal a system of values which rules life in the present. That system of values dictates attitudes and reflects itself in behaviour. For example, neither the young man who may or may not have done the shooting, nor the old men who were shot at, were free agents. They both followed interests growing out of the values of rural life. Sometimes, as in this case, these interests conflict. If open fighting is not to tear life asunder, ways must be found to resolve the conflict, to find a formula of agreement, as the diplomats say.

I have tried in the last of my two examples to show you something of the movements of this sort and something of the agreement which can be reached. The two examples have pointed along the same road; they point to a life with its own laws and its own controls. If we are to see in 'old customs' more than mere *curiosa*, we must reach this life and reduce it to understanding.

II

Countrymen at Work

To bring you closer to the way of life we glimpsed through the window of old custom, I must try to clothe it in flesh and blood. It will not do to make the mistake of etherealizing it. Men everywhere face the same first necessities; they must live; they must feed, clothe and shelter themselves.

My subject, then, is the countryman at work. How does he make his livelihood in the Irish countryside? What is the work he does, and what are his incentives and rewards? Economic interpretations of history, sociology, anthropology are the fashion. What understanding can an economic inquiry yield us?

The first task in such an inquiry is to clear away the ground one is to examine. To look at the work of the countryman of rural Ireland demands dipping into the economics of the whole Free State. The countryman occupies an important place which must be recognized. It should not be discouraging that the task involves recourse to cold statistics. After all, the greatest array of numbers is a mere count of some sort of human activity; one can remember the living beings behind them. In the search for the countryman, one can break through census records and production figures to find him pursuing his daily and annual round.

The task is simplified immensely by the fact that in 1926 the Free State Government undertook a complete census of the country. In the tables prepared there, the countrymen distinguish themselves in a variety of ways. They are the most numerous group in the country. Out of nearly three million inhabitants, one million eight hundred thousand, or 63 per cent, live in rural areas, outside cities and towns. Not all these country-dwellers are farmers, of course, but the vast majority are. Fifty-one per cent of all occupied persons, male and female, in southern Ireland work at agriculture.

But these agriculturalists are not all alike, of course. Distinctions appear among them which are important to an understanding of the countryman. For example, the farms on which they work differ widely in size. Relative proportions of small and large farms vary with different parts of the country, but nevertheless small farms predominate in all Ireland. A farm over 200 acres is a rarity, comparatively speaking; most of them do not reach 100 acres. Thirty or fifty acres is the average size.

When one looks at the numbers of people these farms support, however, the small holdings come forward much more strongly. There are many more persons supported upon farms under thirty acres than there are on farms over fifty. In fact, one could almost say 'the smaller the farm the greater number of persons it supports'. The plurality of Irish farmers support themselves upon farms averaging from fifteen to thirty acres in area. Almost eight of every ten persons working in agriculture live by small-farm production.

By our standards, a farm under thirty acres or even under fifty acres is very small. So it is regarded in Ireland. When I call the Irish countryman a small farmer, I am following standards the Irish use themselves. Yet, to deal with the life of the small farmers is to deal with that of the single largest group on the land.

Furthermore, that group is concentrated in the west and south of Ireland. Historical and economic currents have massed the population in the more rugged 'mountainy' regions of south and west. A county of the rich central plain, such as Meath, where large farms are most numerous, has a density of about fifty persons per square mile. But a poorer, mountainous county such as Mayo, where small farms are very numerous indeed, supports seventy-five persons per square mile or an almost 50 per cent greater density.

But do those who support themselves by small farms form a true category? Are they a group unto themselves, or are they a numeration meaningless for the student of human behaviour? Statistics have a way of revealing real categories in life, but they also send one upon many false scents. One must use them with proper care. In such a case as this, care consists in discovering correlations and fitting them into wholes. For example, one learns little or nothing of various kinds of human beings if one counts only single characteristics. On the other hand, if one counts a wide variety of numerable features and finds one human group distinguishing itself again and again within this wide variety, one is justified in thinking one is dealing with a class of which the individuals are instances.

So it is with the economic data in the Irish records. The small farmers do appear as a true category. They reveal themselves in the cold figures as a class with habits of life of its own, different in kind and in quantitative expression from all others.

Rather than delay over the reasoning which leads to this conclusion, I should prefer to recite the distinguishing marks in the economic sphere.

First, it is clear that the small farmers practise a type of agriculture all their own. Their products differ widely from those of the large farmers, sometimes in kind, sometimes in proportion. The large farmer is a cattleman, a stockman. The small farmer is typically what we have come to call in this country 'a subsistence farmer'. Both depend primarily upon livestock, for Ireland is a country of grass and pasturage, depending less upon tillage than any other European land. But their economies are quite distinct. The small farmer cultivates a 'garden' of oats, rye, potatoes, cabbage and turnips, and devotes his pasture and the hay of his fields to milch cattle. He sells his cows' increase each year. He keeps large numbers of hens and a few pigs. But the milch cow is the centre round which this economy revolves. Nearly all he raises he consumes at home; his family and his farm animals take the greater part of his produce. It is only his surplus and his annual crop of calves which break out of the circle of subsistence and in so doing bring him the only monetary income he receives.

In all this he differs considerably from the big farmer, particularly the so-called 'rancher' of Irish agriculture. The big farmer is primarily a producer of beef. He concentrates upon the production of fat cattle; he depends upon a monetary market in which to dispose of his fattened stock. Upon this market he relies for the supplies which feed himself and his labourers. If he is wealthier and much more of a man of business, he is also nearly entirely dependent upon the whims of price and demand.

Naturally, then, the small farmer and big farmer play quite distinct roles in the economics of exchange, distribution and commerce. The small farmer disposes of his cattle, usually calves of his own breeding, quite differently. He sells this surplus to the dealer, the middleman, the big farmer. As calves grow up they move from the small farm to the large. It is the large farmer who grazes them until they are ready for the English table. Consequently, the local cattle fair is still the small farmer's mart, as it was in the middle ages. The big farmer, on the other hand, sells direct to shippers and exporters. In this system, which represents an immense cattle trade within Ireland, moving cattle endlessly from west to east, from small farms to ranches, and on to their final market in England, the big farmer acts, partly at least, as a commercial middleman or 'processer'. In many ways the 'economic war' with England, which the de Valera government is waging today in an effort to wean Ireland from its dependence upon an English market, is necessarily an attack upon the big farmer. . . .

With all this, it is natural that the small farmers should be different consumers from the rest. They live upon a different diet. They eat very little meat, confining themselves to bacon and occasional poultry. Eggs are a great staple and the potato has only slowly retreated from its place of honour, though the countryman makes sure he shall not allow it to betray him as it did in the time of the Famine. Milk, especially in the form of butter, is consumed more than in any European country. All this the small farmer raises at home. Bread and tea, English invaders of the last century, are now the commonest diet of all, and represent the one staple which he must buy off the farm. This last he shares with the big farmer and the townsman, but otherwise he buys little of the meats and the shop products which fall to the lot of townsman and big farmer.

Neither type of farmer has much use yet for mechanized agriculture as we know it; for both are cattlemen. Nevertheless, the small farmer differs again in the tools he uses. He is the one who clings to hand tools; in poorer districts he must rely upon spade, flail, and scythe. The size of his farm and the poor quality of his land confine him to the manual tools.

Lastly, big farmers and small farmers work their lands quite differently. On the big farm, the farmer-owner uses hired labour. On the small farm, the owner relies upon the united efforts of his family. The countryman's subsistence farming is a family economy in which all members of the family take part—sons, daughters and other relatives. He differs completely in this regard from the large farmer, who is an employer and whose hands are wage earners.

This recitation of the distinguishing marks of peasant economics serves a purpose. It reveals in a roundabout manner what sort of livelihood it is that the countryman wrests from his land. He works a small farm with the help of his family. He raises a small garden of potatoes and a few other foodstuffs which feed both himself and his beasts, which beasts feed him in their turn. He need go to town only for clothing and sundries, for flour and tea, and to sell at the fairs the calves and yearlings which bring in his principal monetary income and provide thus for whatever he cannot produce at home. These cattle go to big farmers, ranchers and shippers; and with the sale his participation in trade and commerce, in 'business', is finished except for his account with the shopkeeper (and in late years, the creamery). As you can well imagine, it is a livelihood little connected with the outside world, and now that agrarian reform has made him full owner of his holding, it is little open to disturbance from the outside.

This is the external view of the small farm. It is the view that usually satisfies the economist. But if one probes deeper and looks at the small farmer's livelihood from within, a fuller picture appears.

That the small farmer is a family man even at work

is important for the study of human behaviour. Eight
out of ten people working in agriculture in Ireland
work not for wages and salaries but by virtue of their
family relationship. The work a man does and the
directions he gives and receives take form within a
social group. That fact yields an opportunity for the
anthropologist. Here, in a modern country, is an economy in which there are other controls on labour than
those we know—money, contracts, individual profit.
To understand these controls is to reach at least one
nucleus of the countryman's way of life.

In County Clare, as in all rural Ireland, the small
farmer's family lives upon the holding it works. As a
rule, the farmhouse is an isolated building standing
upon its own ground and forming an integral part of
the holding. This is the familiar type of farm we know;
Meizen calls it the *Einzelhof*. There are many other
types of settlement in Ireland: villages whose fields
lie round about in somewhat the fashion of the Rus-
sian *mir*; striping fields; and the crazy-quilt pattern
of 'rundale'; but the *Einzelhof* has won out historically.
Anyway, whatever the type of holding, the farm family spends its entire life upon it: sleeping, eating, giving birth and dying there, and sallying forth every day
for work. Whether or not there is a topographic identity between house and land, there is a social one. The
countryside knows the farm as a unit. The farm shares
the name of the family working it. It is inalienably
associated with them.

Since cattle play so large a part in rural economy,
it is natural that this unit should be known and judged
as 'the place of so many cows'. For in Clare the land
is valued for its pasture. It is divided into 'field' for
grazing, and 'meadow' where the grass is cut for hay,
and 'garden', the small tillage plot. In mountain areas,
it may also include rough mountain grazing, called

'mountain', and wherever possible, it includes a 'bit of bog' for 'turf' for the year's fuel. <u>When a small farmer tells you he 'has the place of four cows'</u> he sums up this sort of farm, judging it for its ability to support himself and his family in the country manner and to give pasture to four milch cows. In the phrase he epitomizes rural economy.

Ordinarily the house opens directly into the 'haggard', as the farmyard is called. There in the haggard are the cabins in which cattle are housed and the various sheds and stalls, often built into the masonry of the house itself. In them, farm machines, tools and carts are kept and crops and seed are stored. Hens and other poultry roam at will through the haggard and are housed there, and in one of the sheds pig or pigs find their quarters. The winter's supply of fodder stands there in the form of the great hayrick. The straw-covered pit of turnips and mangels, not far away, will serve for men and cattle; and the turf-rick is near at hand. As for the house itself we have already looked inside, in our search for the west room.

The family with which this unit is associated centres its activity round house and haggard. Even for the men, whose work lies primarily in field, garden and meadow, work centres round the house for a good part of the year. If I give you a sketch of this activity as my co-workers and I saw it day after day in several rural communities in Clare, I hope to throw its general features into relief. Following the countryman at his work, we can learn what his role is, what determines it, and what keeps him to it; we can see its controls and the organization of labour it entails.

The first duty of the farm family's day falls to 'the woman of the house'. Before the others are up, she rakes together such live ashes as remain in the slaked turf fire, puts down new sods, and rekindles the blaze.

Then she hangs the kettle on the hook over the hearth, making ready for the first tea of the day. All day long the kettle will hang there, for at any moment she must be ready to serve a cup of tea to husband, children and visitors. With the first tea comes breakfast: bread, eggs and milk.

By the time breakfast is over, the household is ready for its workaday life. The men are up and dressed for the day's tasks, and the farm wife and mother who serves them and stands by unwilling to sit down till they have had their fill, has begun her daily round. She takes her place later with her daughters and young children who help her throughout the day.

But familiar housework is not the whole of the woman's duty. Her work takes her beyond the house door. After breakfast she takes the milk buckets and goes to milk the cows in the sheds. This is merely one of many trips she makes out into the haggard, for fuel, for water, and to feed the animals and poultry. Milking over, she must not rest, for the whole process of converting milk to butter is her charge. She is an expert at the churn.

Her human charges fed, she must feed the animals in their turn. The full-grown cattle and the horse are not her charge, but she must tend calves and pigs and fowl. Milk and potatoes must be prepared for them all.

Before noon, she hangs a second kettle from the hook. This time she fills it with potatoes for the family. In season, she will add white cabbage, and a portion or two of bacon or salt pork. By the time this is ready the men will be in from the fields impatient for their dinner.

For the men have not been idle. The farmer-father and husband wakes his sons, inspects the cattle and horse, if there is one, and gives them hay and water. If the day is fine, he sallies forth to the fields; if not, and the weather confines him to house and haggard, he has still plenty to do, in building walls, repairing and making machine parts, harness and tools.

Dinner unites the family for the first time since breakfast. Only children of school age are absent and their share of the meal is saved till later. As before, the women and children do not eat till the men have finished. But as the women serve, they all talk about the experiences of the day. It is the chief time of general family conversation. Only the children are silent, for in rural Ireland a well-behaved child is a silent one.

After dinner, work begins anew. For the women chores are much the same as in the morning. Should routine duties come to a pause, there is still plenty to do. Washing, mending, knitting must be done; and their hands are never idle.

The great staple, bread, is baked daily, upon the 'griddle' at the hearth. The women may bake at any time, and even late in the evening when the family is gathered round the fire, their last task may be to bake for supper of bread and tea.

At four in the 'evening', as the countryman divides the day, children arrive from school, to be fed and questioned. For they are important purveyors of news. Later, the men are home from the fields, driving the cattle home, bedding them for the night. The woman must serve supper and milk the cows, bringing the milk in to separate. But though her day is over with the separating, she may not sit idly with the men for long beside the evening's fire. Children, knitting, and baking can still be attended to; tradition and proverb demand that 'one woman in the house be always working'.

Work round house and haggard is continuous; it varies little from season to season. It involves a continuous activity by which the household group orders its life and fulfils its first needs in the midst of a carefully patterned regularity of habit. What variation there is, is itself confined to a narrow range. Certain chores are divided among days of the week, but they show nothing of the swift change of a Solomon Grundy. A farmer's wife of Clare divided her week more rigidly in describing it than she did in practice. "On Monday", she said, "I do the washing, on Tuesday the ironing, on Thursday I make butter, on Friday to market, on Saturday I get ready for Sunday, and on Sunday I go to mass and do as little as I can." Really it is only on Sunday that any change seriously alters the daily round; for the country-people are strict sabbatarians, at least regarding work.

Work on the 'land' beyond the haggard and the house is less restricted. It has a greater range over the farm and offers a wider variety of tasks round the year. There is a wider freedom of choice among tasks as well. Soil and climate are just as insistent as is the household, but they do not force such narrow regularities.

Yet each season brings a task the farmer must perform. Custom and rivalry in the community restrict him as well. He is in fact less free to choose the date of sowing than his wife the hour of dinner. Long-established tradition and ancestral experience imprint upon his mind the best dates for planting, for reaping, for harrowing, for breeding cattle, and so forth. The farmer is caught, willingly of course, in a mesh of rivalries, competitions, condemnations, which binds him the more strongly to the community's patterning of his yearly round.

The seasonal rhythm of farm work reaches its low in winter. On bitter wet days little can be done beyond the haggard wall, as we have noted. All the many tasks of patching and repair are men's work, they fall to the farmer-father and his sons. The annual round is theirs, as the daily one belongs to the women.

For the countryman, the Christmas season, from the beginning of Advent to the Epiphany or 'Little Christmas', is the dead of winter. All farm work is at a standstill. The farmer is free to devote the season to holiday. Outside the weather is unsettled, a cold rain falling on the sodden fields. For him the year has stopped and is waiting to renew its forces.

With the Epiphany, the succession of bitter wet days does not end, but holiday does. One's mind turns to the earnest work of the year to come. The farmer plans his spring planting. On drier days he can clean ditches and drains; he can lay in seed and repair machines. In the evenings, conversation on visits and at home revolves round the coming planting and calving, and traditional experience goes from mouth to mouth. In fact, it is the time for all new plans, for it is Shrovetide, the season of match-making and marriage.

St. Bridget's Day, February 1, marks the beginning of spring. For St. Bridget promised every second day thereafter would be 'hard'. The return of the 'hard' days of wind and clear weather herald the land's drying-off. Through February and March, gardens must be prepared, potatoes planted, fields made ready for the return of the cattle to them. Each 'hard' day is more than welcome, for then work in the fields can go on. By St. Patrick's day, they say in Clare, the potatoes should all be 'down'; after that there still remains much to do, though the worst is over. St. Patrick promised that after his day *every* day would 'come hard'.

Through the rest of the spring, work is at its most intense. Potatoes must be 'stirred' and 'landed'; other root crops 'put down'. March and April see the birth of calves and the beginning of the season of greater milk yields and intensified butter-making. Before that in February and March the 'great spring fairs' take place, and the year's buying and selling of cattle must be done.

Then, gradually, with the return of warm weather and the drying-off of the land, Irish summer begins. May is often the first summer month. Soon the bogs are dry enough for cutting the year's supply of turf and for stacking it to dry under the summer warmth at the bog's edge.

Once the turf is cut and stacked, the first fruits of the farmer's labour begin to appear. The first crop is cabbage, which was planted at odd times very early. It is practically the only green of the diet and old people remember June or July *an chabáiste*, 'the hungry month', when a delayed potato crop might condemn them to a month or more of semi-starvation upon cabbage. Today new varieties of potatoes mature as early as June. But the mature potatoes mark no harvest; they are turned out of the ridges with spade and plough as they are needed.

The first true harvest, and the most important one of the year, is the haymaking. Mowing begins in late July or early August. The haymaking is a race against time and rainy weather. Every effort must be bent to mow, rake, dry and stack the grasses, first in small haycocks, then in the great hayrick in the haggard, before rain brings rot to the lush crop. The farmers speak of it aptly when they call it 'saving the hay'.

Corn crops, oats and rye, come in next, and then through September, October and November the other roots, mangels and turnips, must be 'pulled'. Turf must be brought down to the haggard from the bog-ricks; and everything made ready for man and cattle for the coming winter. Autumn fairs bring a new high in buying and selling cattle; and with the last of them, winter sets in again and Advent has returned. In late November the farmer may turn over his gardens with the plough, to prepare them for the spring. As he follows the furrow, he can look back upon a year ended and forward upon a new one to begin.

Yet, unvarying as this yearly round is, and much as the recurrent patterns of work in garden, meadow and field follow the farmer year after year, from boyhood to death, this work—man's round—is freer and more various, even perhaps more arduous, than woman's. We must remember this difference. It reflects an important dichotomy between the sexes in the organization of labour.

We can see this dichotomy even when the group works as a unit. At various crucial points in the annual round we have just followed, the whole family bends to the tasks at hand together. At potato planting, turf-cutting and haymaking, one can see them working in unison. Even the young children contribute their share to the common rhythm of the task. Yet the woman's role is separate. It is auxiliary; the simpler, less arduous tasks fall to her. The heavier work and command of the enterprise rests with the men. The plough, the harrow, the mower, the scythe, the spade and the turf-cutting *slán* are regarded as masculine implements. The attitudes of the countryside forbid a woman's using them. In the same way, they heap ridicule upon the thought of a man's interesting himself in the feminine sphere, in poultry, or in the churning.

Immemorial folklore bolsters this division. The woman is unlucky to masculine enterprises, for instance: it is dangerous to see a woman on the road to the fair. Likewise, man is dangerous to the woman's work. If he so much as takes his lighted pipe out of the

house while she is churning, he may 'take the butter',
through fairy magic.

In this dichotomy, of course, the male sphere bears
higher value. But dichotomy implies no derogation.
Man's role and woman's role are complementary; both
are indispensable patterns of skill without which the
farm family cannot live. And for that reason each is
reciprocal to the other. Each feels a right to expect
good work from the other, in his or her proper sphere.
A good husband is a skilful farmer; a good wife is a
skilful, willing household worker and auxiliary field
hand. The family makes its way through a nice adjustment of these reciprocal roles. A small farmer of mid-
Clare describes the situation in his own words:

"Here is something I want to tell you and you can
put it in your head and take it back with you. The
small farmer [in Ireland] has to have an intelligent
wife or he won't last long. He may do for a few years,
but after that he can't manage. You take children's
clothes . . . if she knows how to buy material and
make the clothes she saves a lot of money, and there
are a thousand ways an intelligent woman makes
money." Here his wife interrupted him and asked,
"What about the tillage?" "That's all right," he went
on. "But if it wasn't for the woman the farmer wouldn't
last, and when he is getting a wife for one of his sons,
he should look to a house where there has been an
industrious and intelligent woman, because she has
taught her daughters how to work and that is what is
needed."

Here, then, we have one important control in work.
The division of labour between the sexes arises within
a larger field of interests and mutual obligations. It is
a function of the relationship of husband and wife
within the family.

But it is more, too. The attitudes of the countryside

toward men's work and women's work show that their respective skills are regarded also as integral parts of the personalities of all men and women of the countryman's own kind. Here we can see how strongly social dispositions influence both mind and vocabulary. 'Natural' is a word very frequently on the countryman's lips. Thus, it is 'natural' for a woman to be a better milker, her smaller hands are proof. And it is laughably 'unnatural' that a man should bother about the sale of eggs. This division is embedded in tradition, too. Luogh still tells a humorous old tale of the spades, men's tools, that used to work of themselves in the olden days, till a woman forgot to say "God bless the work" to them. This division is bolstered in magic, too, for the 'coulter of a plough', that masculine implement, can bring back the butter the fairies have taken.

The division of labour between the sexes is not the only important division within the countryman's pattern of farm work. Work is divided just as much upon the basis of age. Within the masculine sphere, male family members divide the practice of masculine techniques. Within the feminine sphere, there are similar divisions.

Let us look at the men at their work. The father and husband is normally owner and director of the enterprise. The farm and its income are vested in him. The farm bears his name in the community and sons are spoken of as his 'boys'. In the draining of a field or the sale of cattle at a fair, the sons, even though fully adult, work under their father's eye, and refer necessary decisions to him.

But this relationship is much more than economic. Perhaps the best way of describing it is to trace its development. The child forms part of the productive unit which is his own family. His growing up is also an apprenticeship. He learns the techniques which will make him a full-fledged member of his class; but there is no divorce between technical and non-technical training. All he learns fits him for one end— to become a farmer-father-husband in a family of his own.

The child sees his father as owner, director and principal worker of the farm. From his example, he learns which are men's tasks and he learns to value the skills they demand. In family deliberations he learns, too, the nice balance between the needs of household and land. It is true he learns these techniques in a narrow school; his father makes sure that he does not deviate from the right and traditional pattern, which folklore, adage and the censure of the village support. But he learns well, by example, competition and practice.

This process is the daily experience of many years; it is very gradual and is embedded in traditional social life. The boy's first duties, as soon as he can speak and walk, are to run on petty errands to neighbours and near-by friends. Until he is seven and passes through first communion, his place is in the house with the women, and he shares the same bed with his sisters. After that year, he leaves his mother's apron strings, and is slowly drawn into men's ways; he is thrown more and more with his elder brothers and sleeps with them henceforward. In remote regions he takes off girl's clothing for the first time; for girl's clothing has protected him from the fairies, they say. Both socially and economically he is becoming a male, but his male status is still very little. By the time he is ten or eleven, he is brought home from school when needed to take part in the important agricultural work of the year. But not until he passes confirmation and leaves school, usually at the same time, does he take on full men's work and assume men's clothing. Even then, as he reaches maturity, and takes on more and more the heavy tasks of the farm, he never escapes his father's direction. Only when his father makes over the farm to him, at death or at his own marriage, can he assume command, and with it full adult status.

Economic apprenticeship is thus a process of conditioning within the family. But there is no separation of economic and non-economic spheres. The father's direction of the enterprise coincides with his dominant, controlling role as parent and adult; the boy learns work as he learns manhood.

Also, the child grows up within the full complex of life within the farm family. His first petty errands are a mere incident in the relationship he builds up with his parents and brothers. He learns not only his work but the whole code of conduct which constitutes the folkways of his class, at their hands. This conduct is itself part of his relation to them. It ranges all the way from the errands he runs for his superiors in the family to the learning of his prayers and the development of the sentiments which make sexual behaviour of any kind an offence, and of that within the family, incest.

Consequently, in so well-knit a group, the command which his father (and his mother) exercises over the son in farm work is only one aspect of that control. His subordination continues as long as his father lives. Even though the major work of the farm devolves upon the son and his brothers, they have no control of the direction of farm work nor the disposal of the farm's income. I say the son and his brothers, for all the sons are equal in this subordination; rural Ireland knows neither primogeniture nor junior right. As long as they remain at home upon the farm they share this status equally.

The behaviour that reflects this state of affairs can be readily observed. Sons go to market and fair from the time they are ten or twelve, but they buy or sell little if anything. Father and sons can be seen together at the local markets, but it is the father who does the bargaining. Their attitudes are in agreement with this arrangement. Once I asked a countryman about it at a potato market in Clare. He explained he could not leave his post for long because his full-grown son wasn't well enough known yet and was not yet a good hand at selling. If a son in Luogh and other Clare communities wants a half-crown to go to a hurley match, he must get it from his father. The son may earn money in employment off the farm, on the roads, or as a labourer, but even then he is expected to contribute everything he receives to the household, as long as he remains on the farm. Very often, as the author saw in Luogh, in work on land division, the old fellows will walk to the pay-off to collect for themselves the wages their sons have earned.

You will say, perhaps, that all this has a very familiar ring; it is characteristic of closely knit farm families everywhere. So it is, but we are prone to disregard the familiar; we forget that the familiar stuff of life has often more important implications than the exotic. In the Irish countryside we must not undervalue the familiar. For the implications of these factors of family life are the signposts along the road.

In the countryside this subordination of the sons does not gradually come to an end. It is a constant. Even at forty-five and fifty, if the old couple have not yet made over the farm, the countryman remains a 'boy', both in farm work and in the rural vocabulary. In 1933, a deputy to the Dáil raised considerable laughter in the sophisticated Dublin papers when he inadvertently used the country idiom in expressing country realities. He pleaded for special treatment in land division for 'boys of forty-five and older'—boys who have nothing in prospect but to wait for their father's farm. For 'boyhood' in this instance is a social status rather than a physiological state. A countryman complained to me in words which tell the whole story. "You can be a boy forever," he said, "as long as the old fellow is alive."

Had we more time we might devote a long inquiry to this relationship, to its affective content, to the mutual respect and pride of father and son. The Irish countryside values the stern father perhaps more highly than the indulgent one; the peasant father takes great pride in a sturdy successor and competent fellow-worker. Camaraderie and intimacy may not flourish between them; but deeper-felt affections underlie formal respect and gruff command. The Irish mother, compassionate, indulgent, is of course a counterpoise to this stern paternality. She has an emotional role in the balance of reciprocal sentiments as indispensable to the family's existence as the economic role she plays. Freud might illuminate us about the sort of conflicts such a human structure engenders, but he has little to say of the far more important, and more apparent, balance of emotional forces which it entails.

For this balance is the health of a complete social organism. The countryman who occupies boyhood status so long ordinarily does not revolt. His economic dependence galls him perhaps at times, but he cannot regard it as an injustice. That dependence is itself a product of healthy balance. He has expectancies and prospects; father and mother owe him obligations for which he can and does wait; emotional bonds are fiercely strong, for there is little opportunity to diffuse them. The solidarity of his own family is strengthened through competition with other socio-economic units. The endless petty disputes of the countryside over rights of way, boundaries, cattle trespasses, drainages, are much more than defences of property. 'The two grandfathers' of the contestants 'began it' is the usual defence in court. That solidarity is a mountain of strength against the outside world. 'Defending Tim Flanagan's title' is the jocular way of describing armed resistance to eviction in the country districts in Clare. For Tim Flanagan worked a farm with ten strong adult sons; evicting ten armed stalwarts is no small matter for the best of police. Sons and brothers are a better title than the clearest deed.

The controls in farm work, then, are those of a social group—the family. The countryman at work is little concerned with the usual economic categories. He is a family man. He may be the shrewdest of traders and the best of farmers, but what gives him his occupational status, determines his pattern of work, provides his incentive, is a set of dispositions arising in the balanced interests and reciprocal obligations of the social group to which he belongs.

We can test this conclusion. There are a large number of small farms in the countryside worked by what we can call incomplete families. They are worked by spinsters, bachelors, widowers, widows. In such farms the person owning the farm exercises control. A widow, for instance, is helped out by a male relative —brother, nephew or son. The male takes over the tasks which would ordinarily fall to a farm father. Even if the widow retains control of expenditures and disposal of farm goods, the bargaining, buying and selling in such typically masculine enterprises as the cattle fair rests with the man. For instance, in one example which came to my knowledge, a 'landless' young man pleaded successfully to the Land Commission for an addition to his aunt's holding. It was he who carried out the negotiations successfully. The feeling of the community was sufficiently strong to push the young man into a position beyond his status. Some male must represent the aunt and her holding in the outer world. With old bachelors, a nephew moves in and works the farm, but the old fellow keeps strict control, even to regulating sums spent by the nephew for amusement. Where a widower had a small son, the son was taken by a childless sister. She brought him up to inherit her husband's farm, and her brother might marry again. Two spinsters spent their lives on a farm worked by their cousins.

To the country-people, such arrangements, successful enough economically sometimes, are makeshifts, subjects for commiseration. One hears often enough such phrases as these: "It's a hard life she has with only the brother and no husband to help her." "He's all by himself with only his son there on the land, poor fellow." Even government officials nowadays recognize the social value of the full family. A household of father, mother and sons gets preference in land division. The work to be done is the strengthening of the social group; personal enrichment and use of the soil are merely incidental.

Up to this point, I have described the countryman as though he worked in isolation from his fellows. In a measure this is true, for his first duties are to his immediate family. Still, there is a great deal of work which goes on between farms. There is a certain amount of co-operation of an informal kind. Work in the countryside is permeated with a give-and-take of reciprocal aids.

Co-operation of this sort takes many forms. Men lend tools, or work with tools of their own for 'friends' and neighbours, particularly at mowing, spring sowing, harrowing, ploughing. They send along a boy to help whenever the farm needs an extra hand to get its work done quickly. Women pool resources in making

up a tub or firkin of butter or they lend a girl to a
short-handed household. 'Friends' and neighbours
help one another at times of distress, or when a household is short or a crop delayed. Gifts of cattle, food
and labour are made. Or they work together com-
munally, particularly at turf-cutting, oats harvest and
threshing. Here again much of the actual work is done
by the 'boys' lent by their fathers, though the latter
take a hand when necessary. Lastly, there is a great
deal of aid given and received in preparing for ceremonial and social occasions, at christenings, weddings
and funerals.

Once this co-operation was more widespread. Older
people remember the days when 'once if you had a
horse and car you'd have forty or fifty people helping
you with the turf'. Before mowing-machines came in,
ten or a dozen 'friends' would work each other's meadows in turn with the scythe. In that way the slender
resources of the countrymen were pooled; and the
work of life went forward. Nowadays, the small farmer
is better off; he has less immediate need of his fellows.
Nevertheless, he has not forgotten them; in all but the
communities where large farmers have forsaken peasant life for a monetary agriculture, he can and does
rely upon them still. Nowadays, however, the co-
operating groups are smaller; tools are more modern
and better distributed; resources are fuller.

Lending a 'boy' is the commonest form of co-
operation. It goes on constantly, but can best be described in a scene of great activity, such as haymaking. I met it first there, in Luogh, the townland in
which we found the west room. The hay was early
in Luogh in 1933. Harvest began in mid-July. The
weather was just right. Warm dry days had brought
the grasses to maturity, and gave promise of continu-
ing. The families of Luogh set to work to 'save the

hay': mowing it, letting it dry as it lay, and then stacking it, first into small grass cocks, then into the usual six- to eight-foot haycocks. Later, after several weeks, it would be moved into a single great hayrick in the haggard. Now it was a question of mowing, drying and stacking it before rains caught the farmers in midcourse.

There was much interest in every family's progress. The weather and the yields of the meadows drove all other subjects out of conversation. The men felt spurred to work well and quickly; there was a general rivalry in the air. The women were as eager, and brought their children to the meadow's edge, while they worked with their rakes behind the mowers.

About half the families had horse-drawn mowing machines. Those who had them mowed their own meadows, working from earliest morning as long as light held. They worked with the aid of their sons and of boys from the families who had no machines. At each stage of the process a boy not a member of the family gave his labour; he took his place at meals during the day.

His own mowing done, the farmer paid his debt. He took his machine to the farmer whose son had helped him and mowed that man's meadow. In one instance, a youngish farmer mowed the meadows of three others. In another, a farmer mowed for two others. Certain meadows in Luogh were full-handed enough to do without extra hands; but in five cases, though mowing and stacking took a very long time and they were obviously short of hands, no help was given. Two of these cases were bachelors, who lived alone; two more were 'strangers'.

Here was an important agricultural operation undertaken by the small local community in which provision was made for effective co-operation over and above the usual family economy. It was no isolated instance; it is immemorial practice in Luogh. In fact, during late July and August the entire small farm population of Clare can be seen at work.

There was no monetary payment involved in this work. In the country surrounding Luogh, the only hired labour to be seen worked the meadows of a large farmer, a cattleman with over 300 acres. He did not co-operate; in fact, his whole life was cut out of a different cloth.

This co-operation is woven deeply into the countryman's habit and sentiment. Questioning in the life of the present soon brought out the base upon which it rests. In every case an extended-family relationship was involved. The countryman is a family man in this co-operation with his fellows, as well as in his work at home. Carey, who mowed for Denis and Seamus Moloney and for Brian MacMahon, was second cousin to each of them. Peter Barrett was first cousin and uncle respectively to the two farmers whose meadows he mowed. The 'boys' who worked Carey's and Barrett's meadows were also relatives; they were sons of the kinsmen for whom Carey and Barrett had mowed.

So it went over the townland. No man had mowed for all his relatives, that was not necessary. One man had mowed not for a relative, but for a boon companion. Furthermore, the bachelors, whom no one had helped, had been able to help no one. The two 'strangers', who had moved into the townland, in one case fifty years before, in the other thirty, had no relatives 'on this side'.

The small farmers of Luogh explained their co-operation in their own general terms. They call it 'cooring' in the brogue. The word is the Irish *comhair*, meaning aid, partnership, and alliance. They explained their 'cooring' in terms of the 'friendliness' of the place. Their answer was that they "had right to help their friends", or in a more general statement, "country people do be very friendly, they always help one another".

Now, 'have right' and 'friend' are both expressions in the brogue. Like so much of that rich English dialect, for it is a true dialect with an ancient history, both words translate Gaelic idiom. A 'friend' is a relative. To 'have right' expresses an obligation, a duty and the traditional fitness of an act. It is an anglicization of an Irish *tá cóir orm*, 'the obligation is on me'. The countryman is explaining his acts as part of the traditional reciprocities of sentiment and duty which make up his system of kinship.

This fact strikes one the more strongly when one finds him describing other traditional acts of obligation to kindred in exactly the same terms. Aid lent and duties performed at wedding and funeral are felt to be in the same category as co-operation in farming. Thus a farmer of my acquaintance could say of a cousin: "He is the best friend we ever had; we can make bold on him. Johnny sent down a cow and calf worth £12 to us and didn't want anything for it." And he could go on in more general terms: "Everybody's friends in the country here are very good to you; they lend you a horse with the hay, or a boy going to the fair, or they send down to help when somebody dies with you". It is part of the 'friendliness' owed one's kinsmen to make up and serve food at wakes and weddings, to dig the grave, to carry the coffin, to keen over the dead. This conduct is reciprocal; 'friendliness' implies mutual obligation. One countryman gave me as his reason for going to the funeral of a second cousin: "I have right to go, they always come over to this side". When in Luogh a man's wife died and his sister took over the child, she did the 'friendly' thing that she 'had right to do'. In the very same terms a man 'made bold' upon his brother-in-law to lend him a son to help drive cattle to the fair, as the brother-in-law 'had right' to do.

In fact, failure to fulfil the pattern of conduct demanded by the obligations of 'friendliness' may bring punitive action on the part of the aggrieved kindred. We have seen this before in the story of the old man's curse in the first lecture. In a part of Clare, not many miles from Luogh, a small farmer neglected his garden and forced his father-in-law to send up loads of potatoes for his wife's support. He was finally beaten up one night in his own house by his irate in-laws. Ordinarily, perhaps failure leads rather to an estrangement; it holds one up to general condemnation by the whole community. Persistence in failure leads to social death; the recluse is greeted by no one, not even his 'friends'.

But fulfilment entrenches one in social life. The obligations extend to visiting and hospitality, the countryman's great virtue. 'A sup of tea' is 'put down before' the countryman who is travelling to town, or to the fair, or only making the evening *cuaird* or visit. The obligations pattern good-fellowship and holiday, for friends treat one another when they meet near a pub. In fact one countryman complained to me that he dreaded the fair day, for he must drink up all his profits with his friends, but others seem to manage their obligations better.

And lastly, the obligations of kinship are a bulwark against disaster. The Johnny mentioned above sent the cow down when it was badly needed. If you have read the book from the Blaskets called *The Islandman*, you remember that the Islandman might not marry the girl of his choice because she was a mainlander and the friends she would bring him would be too far away from Great Blasket when he needed aid. In the system of reciprocal duties which surround kinship, much of the strength of the countryside against external destruction and internal disaster is explained.

We have followed the countryman a long way. In watching him at his work, we have begun to recognize the outlines of the way of life which is his. He is a subsistence farmer, as we now call the peasant, but he is more. He is part of an intricate social system which patterns his life along definite channels, which brings him rewards, gives him incentives, and deals its own punishments. The traditional patterns of old custom have a place in this system; folklore surrounds it as in the dichotomy between men's and women's work. But tradition is not all its secret; it is a living structure with a balance and a growth of its own. It is built out of the behaviour and the sentiments men and women have toward one another. Farm work is merely one expression of the balanced pattern of relations between human beings. We now must see what that structure is and how it maintains itself.

III

The Family and the Land

Balance, pattern, system, structure, may perhaps seem formidable terms. They may seem too heavy and too prosaic to do justice to the countryman's way of life. Or again, they may strike you as too formal; for what I name with them is compounded of a thousand personal intimacies. Yet no other terms represent so well the fluid realities of social life. I do not mean that there are not others that might not serve as well. I mean only that the anthropologist cannot use the others; for they are infused with the very emotions which he must coldly dissect. The others are sacred to the patriot and the poet; they are tabu to the uninspired.

I traced the Irish countryman at his work in the last lecture. He finds his role in life and farm labour made for him in the groups to which he belongs. His activities, incentives and rewards take shape within the habitual expectancies and mutualities which make up the pattern of his family. A great deal of his activity beyond the farmhouse door derives from the reciprocities of his system of kinship. Looked at externally, as we are looking at him, he is a unit in a balance of human relationships. He may never attain such a view of himself, of course; from his point of vantage, he is a staunch 'friend' and a loyal son and brother. The balance, which we can see objectively, is to him a deep personal intuition.

Now I face the question: How does this balance

maintain itself? What does it imply for him? The point round which the balance revolves is marriage. As we have seen, the west room takes its aura from a change which comes over the parental couple; the 'boy' reaches adult status when he marries and inherits the farm. The family and the land are both involved in this crucial reorganization.

Country marriage in Ireland follows an ancient and widespread pattern. It is called 'match-making' and it is the sort of *mariage de convenance* involving parental negotiations and a dowry which is nearly universal in Europe. In Ireland its importance is such as to make it the crucial point of rural social organization.

To describe the match one has to sink one's teeth into the countryman's way of life. For the match is made up of many things. It unites transfer of economic control and advance to adult status. It is the only respectable method of marriage and the usual method of inheritance in the Irish countryside. It is embedded in the Gaelic tongue, in joke and story, and in folklore.

A match usually begins when a farmer casts round for a suitable wife for one of his sons. The son to be married is to inherit the farm. The farmer has full power to choose among his sons. A hundred years ago, before famine, clearances and land reform, all the sons and daughters could hope to be provided for on the land. Such a situation is still an ideal, but little more. One cannot subdivide one's holding any longer, and new farms are hard to get. Today the farmer looks forward, ordinarily, to 'settling' only one son 'on the land'.

"When a young man is on the lookout for a young lady", a farmer of Inagh in mid-Clare told me, "it is put through his friends for to get a suitable woman for him for his wife. It all goes by friendship and friends and meeting at public-houses." I think we can remem-

ber from the last lecture what he means. Getting
married is no carefree, personal matter; one's whole
kindred help, even to suggesting candidates.

"The young man", the farmer goes on, "sends a
'speaker' to the young lady and the speaker will sound
a note to know what fortune she has, will she suit, and
will she marry this Shrove? She and her friends will
inquire what kind of a man he is, is he nice and steady.
And if he suits, they tell the speaker to go ahead and
'draw it down'. So then he goes back to the young
man's house and arranges for them to meet in such a
place, on such a night and we will see about it." With
this, the first step in the delicate negotiations is safely
passed.

The Inagh farmer goes on: "The speaker goes with
the young man and his father that night, and they
meet the father of the girl and his friends or maybe
his son and son-in-law. The first drink is called by the
young man; the second by the young lady's father.

"The young lady's father asks the speaker what fortune do he want. He asks him the place of how many
cows, sheep, and horses is it? He asks what makings
of a garden are in it; is there plenty of water or spring
wells? Is it far in from the road, or on it? What kind
of house is in it, slate or thatch? Are the cabins good,
are they slate or thatch? If it is too far in from the
road, he won't take it. Backward places don't grow
big fortunes. And he asks, too, is it near a chapel and
the school, or near town?"

The Inagh countryman could pause here; he had
summarized a very long and important negotiation.

"Well," he went on, getting to the heart of the matter, "if it is a nice place, near the road, and the place
of eight cows, they are sure to ask £350 fortune.
Then the young lady's father offers £250. Then maybe
the boy's father throws off £50. If the young lady's

father still has £250 on it, the speaker divides the £50 between them. So now it's £275. Then the young man says he is not willing to marry without £300— but if she's a nice girl and a good housekeeper, he'll think of it. So, there's another drink by the young man, and then another by the young lady's father, and so on with every second drink till they're near drunk. The speaker gets plenty and has a good day."

The farmer paused here again; for the match is developing marvellously. "All this is one day's work," he continued. "After this, they appoint a place for the young people to see one another and be introduced. The young lady takes along her friends, maybe another girl, and her brother and her father and mother. The young man takes along his friends and the speaker.

"If they suit one another, then they will appoint a day to come and see the land. If they don't, no one will reflect on anybody, but they will say he or she doesn't suit. They do not say plainly what is wrong.

"The day before the girl's people come to see the land, geese are killed, the house is whitewashed, whiskey and porter bought. The cows get a feed early so as to look good; and maybe they get an extra cow in, if they want one." He said this last slyly, for to pretend to own more stock than one really has, is an unfair trick in the bargaining.

"Then next day comes the walking of the land. The young man stays outside in the street, but he sends his best friend in to show the girl's father round, but sure the friend won't show him the bad points.

"If the girl's father likes the land he returns, and there will be eating and drinking until night comes on them. Then they go to an attorney next day and get the writings between the two parties and get the father of the boy to sign over the land." With the writings, the match is made, and the wedding can go forward.

This long statement, in fact, contains the essence of the whole of match-making. It serves very well as a general guide. A great deal is at stake in this elaborate negotiation. To our eyes, such a way of winning a wife seems very unromantic. It savours a little too much of hard-headed business. We should call a man a cynic who put farm and fortune ahead of personal attractions.

Yet we should be wrong to make such an evaluation of the countryman. The sentiments prompting him, and his expectations, are quite different; they must be understood in their proper setting. In match-making, the interests of all the members of both families are deeply involved. The match is a convention by which they are expressed and realized. We are prone to forget that a living convention can be just as joyous, even more so, in fact, than bohemian revolt.

For example, the heated, formal bargaining quickly summarized by the quotation has deep significance. It effects a necessary and balanced equality between the two families. Superficially, it seems merely a nice adjustment between the farm and fortune. But looked at more closely, it assures many things.

The girl's family know that she will be well provided for. They make sure of it when they 'walk the land'. They make sure their standing in the countryside will not suffer. Fortune and farm must be roughly equivalent. In the scale of rural prestige, each farm is valued against the fortune it can pay out with its daughters and the fortune it can bring in with its inheriting son's wife. In the words of the Inagh countryman quoted: "Backward places do not grow big fortunes". And as the farm is identified socially with the family whose members work it, these dowries measure the family's standing.

On the side of the family receiving the fortune, too, interests are served. The girl's dowry comes to them, to be used for their own purposes. With it, they are assured a competent 'new woman', as they call the new wife and daughter-in-law. She is trained to their position in life and to their own habits and sentiments. Girl and dowry are a fair exchange for prestige and alliance.

But these are not the only values at stake. The 'fortune' in the match is woven into the internal necessities of farm family life.

When agreement is finally reached between the negotiating parties, they go to a solicitor to make up the 'writings', as we saw in the quotation. By this, the countryman means they cast their agreement into legal form. For the 'writings' is a contractual instrument which unites marriage settlement and will. Reforms in land tenure have made it necessary recently to give an age-old custom proper legality, since the transfer of the farm is involved.

In the 'writings' the father of the groom makes over the farm and all its appurtenances to his son. In return, the girl's fortune goes to him. The father also makes provision for his own maintenance and that of his wife. It is his abdication, and like Charles V, he keeps only one monastery out of a vast empire for himself. He usually reserves the right to the 'grass of a cow', his keep, the use of the hearth, and the use of a room in the house. That room is the 'west room' already described, the best in the house. Thus, the cycle of life on the farm is completing itself. He and his wife step down from active command.

In payment for his abdication, he receives the fortune of the girl. A fair arrangement, we should say.

But we should be wrong; it is much more. True to the obligations of his social role, he may not use it entirely for himself. The Irish small farmer does not retire, like the Iowan, to sunny California and the Townsend plan. He must meet the interests of the group. Ordinarily, the other children have been stalwart workers in the farm family corporation. They are not to be 'settled on the land'; some other provision must be made. They may come forward now for their long due reward and their corporate share.

Here the purposes behind the match show themselves again. One daughter is ordinarily married into a near-by farm. The family makes a match for her. With her, of course, goes a fortune equal to that the son's bride brings in. Perhaps, a son may be similarly married into a farm where there are only daughters; even though a *cliamhan isteach*, 'son-in-law going-in', as he is graphically called in Irish, must pay a much larger fortune. He has to overcome the anomaly felt in reversing the usual role of sons and daughters and has to compensate the family for the loss of 'their name on the land'.

But it is a very fortunate farmer indeed who can provide for all his sons and daughters so. Usually, only the heir and one daughter are married and dowered, the one with the farm, the other with the fortune. All the rest, in the words of the Luogh residents, 'must travel'.

Thus, either at the match or in preparation for it comes the inevitable dispersal of the farm family. The unit must break up. Time and change are inevitable in human affairs; only an orderly social mechanism can tame their ravages.

The match provides rural Ireland with this mechanism. It accomplishes the necessary transformation of the family. The balance of interests and duties, of prides and loyalties, hinges upon it.

There are two facets to the change, an external and an internal. The distinction is understandable, it is that between internal constitution and external face. Or better, let us state it in figurative terms. Shakespeare's "All the world's a stage" was profound sociology. Life in organized society is a drama. In the match, even though the marriage of one principal is the theme, the action includes the whole cast. Internally, the action forcibly and finally changes the interrelations of all the characters; externally, the parts they play to the audience alter and grow. The changes must run their course till the action resolves itself in the crystallization of a new situation; and the act is over.

It is this dramatic quality which gives the sociologist and the social anthropologist the right to use such terms as 'structure', 'dynamics' and 'equilibrium'. He has that right in describing the life of the countryman. The match brings changes in dramatic completeness. It forces the relationships of the constituent human beings into a new equilibrium and creates a scaffolding for new behaviours and sentiments.

Let us look at the external change first. The sons and daughters who must travel are forced out of the closely knit group in which they once had their being. Yet, unless they emigrate beyond hope of call, they do not drop out of sight. The sentiments of years of close association do not die out. It has been a matter of pride and duty with the farm father to provide well for his children. Wherever he can, he has found them an opening. He has sent them into the towns, into the shops, the professions, the trades, and into the Church. As in nearly all modern countries today, there is in Ireland a great and constant flow of population from country to city. Much of this is made up of the farm sons and daughters.

Yet, they do not always go to the towns, of course. The farm father tries to settle them on the land round about him, too, as we have seen. In either case, nevertheless, they are not lost to the new family which supplant them on the farm. They are merely removed a single step. They have become 'friends'. They are part of the extended kinship system which stretches from the farmhouse door. They owe the obligations of kindred which we saw in farm work; they are the uncles and their children the cousins of the new generation in the home farm.

Out of this sort of expansion Irish kinship is built. The point of integration is the farm father and mother, whose relinquishment of command forces dispersal. Projected backward and upward through the generations, to common grandfathers and great-grandfathers, this transferred remembrance of the duty and sentiment between father and son unites ever wider circles of descendants in the ties of brotherhood. It provides a scaffolding for the behaviours of 'friendliness' and 'cooring' between members of contemporaneous generations. In it each man has a place, reckoned upon 'blood' as he calls it. With the word, a social structure of interwoven habit patterns and emotional reciprocities gains a mystic force, all the more compelling.

For all its intensity, Irish kinship is no 'clan', as anthropology uses the term. For there are no fast bounds and no rigidities; it is a system of potentialities. It is expansive, rather than restrictive. Both the Gaelic language and the brogue are very chary of kinship terms. One finds no huge vocabulary such as categorizes each Australian blackfellow for his comrades. All the reckonings proceed from the heart of the system; they are appeals to 'blood'. Because of the structural simplicity of the system they are insistent upon membership in a common generation in a common descent. Thus one hears countrymen distinguish between 'my friends' and 'my father's friends', specifying two generational groups. In his own generation, he will make a similar distinction, categorizing with a variety of expressions all those who occupy the same place as he does in descent from a common ancestor. Thus, he embraces ever wider numbers of his contemporaries. For him 'a distant friend' is less to be relied upon than a 'near' one; but the distance he reckons is not that of space. Rather it is that of cousinship.

Though he has no elaborate terminology of kinship in which to enmesh his relatives, the countryman has another weapon, in appeal to common 'blood'. He is no rootless parvenu. Like the medieval Irish annalists, whose kinship system he inherits, he is proud to be an able genealogist. Genealogy permeates his view of man and the world.

He judges himself and his contemporaries by their 'blood'. Like many another people, he makes a *deus ex machina* of this verbal identification. 'Good blood' explains success and high position; 'bad blood' failure and low estate. To insult a man it is enough to suggest he has 'tinker blood' or 'robber blood' in his veins. One damns thus a whole kindred by impugning its descent. Even such a socially undesirable state of affairs as a feud between two angry, warring kindreds can be given a name in accordance with this identification. It is said that 'there is bad blood between them'.

In fairy-tales and folklore the mystic force of common descent is stronger than fate and circumstance. The rightful son and brother, lost or stolen away, is finally restored to the heritage of his blood. For the 'blood' and the 'land' are identified as well. The social mind is not content with half-hearted inclusions. One's blood calls to one's possessions. A particular ancestral line is inseparable from a particular plot of earth. All others are 'strangers to the land'.

But there is, of course, a practical side too. We have seen it already in the account of agricultural co-operation, not, unfortunately, the kind A. E. and Sir Horace Plunkett advocated, but the pattern of centuries of local life. We shall learn more of it when we discuss shops, pubs and fairs. In either of these cases, the kinsmen, the dispersed children, remain within the confines of local life.

The new equilibrium has a place even where emigration removes the dispersed children altogether. The behaviours and sentiments of kinship 'travel' with them. They send back remittances and passage money for nephews and nieces, brothers and sisters. There is a marked tendency for emigration from a local region to perpetuate itself. Sons and daughters of each generation go out to join the members of the last. One little settlement called Cross, on the Loop Head peninsula which juts out from Clare into the Atlantic at the Shannon's mouth, is said locally to be supported by the Shanghai police force. The first man to go is now Chief of Police in the International Settlement there, and many places in the Force have gone to men of Cross.

Such services are part of the same 'friendliness' which sums up the kinship system. And naturally, where kinship is based upon extension, bonds are stronger as the original relationship is closer. Thus a brother is more likely to aid one's self and one's children than is a cousin, though the obligation binds them both. An incident from Luogh will show the human setting in which emigration often takes place. The farmer tells the story himself:

"A fellow named O'Dwyer married to a cousin of the old woman's out of Ballyheline [a neighbouring townland] was home from Australia one summer, looking a fine cut of a man with a great new coat and a fine hat on him. I saw him one day when we were all in Considine's shop for the old-age pension and knew who he was from the pictures of him. [After they had established recognition and struck up a friendship] he asked could he take the boy [my second son] out to Australia with him, and he would put him behind his bar [he had a hotel out there]. I said yes, he could have him.

"After this fellow went back to Australia, he sent over £50 for passage for Seumas. But didn't Seumas' sisters write from Boston and they swearing that if I let their brother go off from them to Australia I'd never hear from them again. So Seumas went out to America to his sisters. I sent back the £50, and sure wasn't it the devil's own work sending it back."

So much for the external change which the match brings. What now can we learn of the internal change and the new internal equilibrium that change brings?

The transfer of the land to the son who marries carries with it a drastic reformation in the relations of the household members who remain. The headship of the parental couple is profoundly modified. The 'old people' move into a new status, that of old age. For both the man and the woman it means an abandonment of power; they are no longer the 'man and woman of the house'.

Where the transition is smooth, father and son continue to work together. One family in Luogh, for example, was regarded as a model of family harmony. It was made up of a young man and his wife and two children and the old couple. But the old man worked by his side, and the son deferred to his judgment. The greatest compliment the neighbours had for them was this: "Look at the Careys; old Johnny gives his boy a hand in everything. You wouldn't know which one has the land."

The introduction of the old-age pension has facilitated this transfer. Originally designed for the support of the aged in an industrial population in England, it has speedily woven itself into the fabric of Irish rural life. Nowadays, the farmer can turn over his land at the age of seventy. In doing so, he divests himself of his property which stands in the way of his receiving the pension. One countryman of my acquaintance sang the praises of the pension in no uncertain terms. His words show clearly that, even with this new source of income at his disposal, the old, abdicating farm father still forms part of the family economic unit. "To have old people in the house", he said, "is a great blessing in these times, because if you have one it means ten bob a week and if you have two it means a pound a week coming into the house. You take a man like O'Donoghue [a neighbour] and every Friday he will go to Corofin to collect his ten bob. He may buy a couple of bottles of porter but he'll spend the rest on things for the household and then come home with a few shillings to go into the common fund."

For the old couple are still very important within the family. Their years of command do not disappear overnight. The change must be handled smoothly. The happiest compromise is that one farmer of Inagh described: "Every morning, even after I was married, I would go to the old man and ask him what I should do for the day, and the old man would say it is now time to do this or that, or the cows should have something done for them, or the garden be prepared. I would go then and spend twenty-thirty minutes doing what the old man said, and then I would go do my own business."

The solution rural Ireland suggests to this problem is deference and respect. There can be no equality between the generations. In the words of one local sage, who could discuss the matter with the experience of a Dorothy Dix: "When the new woman is brought into the house, she may have modern ideas and be hoity-toity about the way to do things. So the old woman and the new woman wouldn't get along. The old man wouldn't say anything but he would light his pipe and go out till the squabble is over. It might get so bad that the old woman would get up and leave, and go live with her daughter some place. She could do this if the daughter's husband's mother were dead, even though the father might still be living in the house.

"But these squabbles are bad things. If the new woman would ask the old person her opinion on how to do this and that there never would be any trouble and the new wife could go ahead and do just as she pleased. Then the old woman would think she was doing it the way that she said. If the daughter-in-law did what she ought, she would do this and treat the old folks nice."

Deference and respect solve the problem, then, but if they do not, it is the older woman who must leave. That this should be the case reflects one great function of farm marriage. The son must cleave to his bride. If the worst comes to the worst, the new family may 'turn the old people out on the side of the road'. Terrible as such an ending would be, it is the necessary one. For the pattern of family and land must continue in the persons of the new man and woman and their children.

This desire is the binding force in the relations of all the household. It is as strong in the old people as in the new couple. The new balance of sentiments finds its expression in the inclusion of the children born to the young man and woman. Like so much of their behaviour, the country-people describe the new ties in terms of the 'help' they afford to the family corporation. And once again, naturally, an economic explanation is all too elliptical. A thoughtful farmer of Inagh generalized the matter in words which show the identity between help in farm work and social reciprocities: "When there are children in the house, the old people are a great help to the mother, because the old woman would nurse the youngsters and see they didn't fall into the fire or something of that nature. The old man would keep on at his work just as long as he was able because it was in the nature of things that he had always done so. The old woman would help in the house. If there was a squabble between the mother and the daughter, the old woman would be more likely to stand up for the daughter. She would also teach her how to do things and have more patience than the mother. The grandfather would show the boy how to do things and would have more patience than the father."

Accordingly, the chief duty of the 'new woman' is to bear children. She succeeds or fails as a supplier of new persons to the family. Only with children can the new balance complete itself and the essential social continuity be assured.

The old couple appraise their daughter-in-law upon her success in this role. The first year of the girl's marriage is a time of apprenticeship. Her work is light. Highly ceremonialized custom grants her an occasional escape back to her own people. Her major duty is pregnancy, and the old couple watch her like a hawk for signs of fertility. All during her child-bearing years the old people will help her, praising her in terms of her increase, and showing as great an interest in the arriving children as she does herself.

One countryman of North Clare put that first year into words: "At first", he said, "the boy's people make much of the new woman. They would hardly let her work at all. This carries on for seven or eight months, and if then the old people don't see evidence of increase of young, they get angry and abuse her. But if they do, they don't let her do any work at all now and are so proud."

In such a situation barrenness is a curse and a disgrace. The husband has every right to express his disappointment and his displeasure. It is a source of shame to him as well. He fails in preserving the continuity of his line upon the land.

One childless woman of Inagh in Clare knew bitterly how much both family and community support these attitudes: "No matter how much money you have," she said, "no matter how good-looking you are, if you don't have children, you are no good. But if you are ugly as the worst and have children, you are all right." Then she went on, to perpetrate an Irish bull, perhaps, but to express the matter very forcibly: "The man wants children just as much as the woman. He is afraid others will tell him he is no good if he hasn't any. Children are the curse of this country, especially if you haven't any."

Nevertheless, there are other ways of ensuring the continuity. They 'keep the name on the land' too, but they are makeshifts at best. These makeshifts transfer control of the land, as does the match. But in each case, they conform to the system of values lying at the centre of the countryman's way of life. They are social detours, ways past the obstacles of adverse circumstance and bad luck.

For instance there used to be, not long ago, what was known as a 'country divorce'. In the old days, they say, a farmer might send a barren wife back to her parents. He could not marry again, of course; Catholic law forbids it. But he could do something just as effective in assuring the family descendants. He could remarry, not in his own person, but in that of his brother. The two men are equivalent in status, why should they not act sociologically as a single individual. Even today this device survives. Thus a farmer of Corofin, in North Clare, could make use of it. Childless after several years, he got a 'country divorce'. Then he gave the land to his brother, in return for a large fortune, on the stipulation that his brother should marry. One brother thus got wife and farm; the other the dowry. The identity of land and family were preserved for another generation.

What other devices are possible has already appeared in what I previously called 'incomplete families'. Nephews, nieces, even grandchildren may be brought in. In time, a match is made for them, and normal succession assured. The former owners move to the 'west room'; they become the old people, and the pattern of a complete farm family unit is restored. To the country-people it is only the 'crabbit' person who will sell the land, and 'go to town and drink the money'. Such conduct is indefensible, and for good reason. It runs counter to every law of kinship and local custom.

But in the case of a young widow, a conflict can arise. The countryside recognizes only dimly, if at all, the right of a woman to hold land in her own person. That does not mean she cannot exercise full control and work the land herself, which she often does. Rather, she is regarded as holding it in trust for a brother or a son of her husband or her father. She cannot alienate it from the patrilineal line to which it belongs. The conflict arises because she herself moves between two such lines; her father's and her husband's.

Consequently, a widow remains upon the farm only if her children are growing up. If they are very young she returns to her father's farm, and a husband's brother takes over. If she is childless, she is hardly regarded as having moved out of her own kindred; she is buried, when she dies, not with her husband but with her father.

Even if she marries, she and her new husband merely hold the land in trust. The second husband and his children are 'strangers to the land'. The rightful heir by blood, whose 'name' is on the land, may turn them out. So strong is the identification. The woman gets the place only as a mother of the family's sons. One must remember that I am not speaking of formal title or legal right. They may be often quite different and run counter to rural values, breeding strife and forcing the aggrieved to seek redress outside the law.

Here, then, is the new equilibrium in the countryman's social life. The match provides a transition between the generations. Within the family unit, it provides for the establishment of a new nuclear group. It makes room for an essential continuity in which all the members may share and round which all their interests may be centred. Externally, it regathers those whom it must disperse. Round this dispersal, the web of kinship can be built. In the persons of the old people moved one step toward death, and in the identifications round them, 'descent' and 'blood' and 'the name on the land', the emotions of human groups can find their nexus.

In this movement, household, land, adult status, economic control, all move together. Marriage is a turning point round which rural life hinges. It is a structural centre. Every tie between human beings is modified. Then, in a new form, they can crystallize again—to give scope for movement, to allow continuities, to habituate human beings to new social places.

The whole of this movement takes place within a frame of human sentiments, ambitions and desires. Emotion lends its force. Convention, habit and the sanctions of public opinion and private anger keep the bounds and punish transgression. Public honour and self-satisfaction reward conformity. Yet, all this is still a primary social adaptation. It is not reasoned; it is made up of the habitual face-to-face contact of human beings and the folkways of the community. Yet, neither does it shut out reason; there is ample play for wits, for intelligence and for self-interest. For there is certainly nothing remote, esoteric or formal within this frame. There are no rules to learn that the countryman does not feel within himself or his fellows.

This rural familism is based upon psychological and physiological realities. Within it, the drives of the human animal find satisfaction. Hunger, reproduction, love and anger, domination and submission—all have a place. But these satisfactions, as you can see, are far from being haphazard. They are carefully patterned and controlled. The conditioning the countryman receives is personal; it is a conditioning to other human beings. It is part of an intricate web of human relationship. It is a balance of personalities in movement, crystalline at moments, fluid at others, and transformed when necessary in regular and orderly fashion.

In the light of a rural life which can be looked upon as a whole system, the peculiarities of Irish population figures take on meaning.

The Free State exhibits a very interesting and peculiar demography. The statistics of population in Ireland are startling, in many ways. Long-continued emigration has brought about an enormous decline in population, at times when most other nations have been increasing rapidly. The enormous exodus which followed the Famine was only the high-water mark of the tide of emigration. The outward flow began long before the Famine and has continued down to the present. Only in 1932, in a time of world-wide depression and immigration barriers, did it come to what may be an end. For the first time for well over a century, more Irishmen returned to their native land than left the country.

Naturally, after so long an emigration, this outward flow of population had become a permanent condition in the life of the nation. In 1926, the censustakers reckoned that 30 per cent of all native-born Irish were then living outside the country of their birth. Put in more intimate terms, this meant, roughly, that every child growing up must expect to see at least three out of every ten of his playmates and companions go beyond the seas. And unlike the Greek or the Sicilian, and many another national, he could not expect them to return. He must lose them permanently.

But this three out of ten is an unfair representation. The country districts have suffered this loss at a much greater rate than the towns. On the whole, the towns have gained over the countryside. The cities, as everywhere else, have swollen at the expense of the rest of the country. The countryside has been the victim of two enormous drains—one, the normal, small farmers' flow from country to town—the other, over-seas. As this group, the small farmers, is overwhelm-ingly the most numerous in the land, the drain has taxed it most.

But the small farmers, the country-people, are the very group who exhibit most strongly another statisti-cal peculiarity. They set the norm for the country in marital statistics. In this, the Irish Free State occupies a unique place. Marriage takes place at a later age than in any other country for which records are kept. Sixty-two per cent of all males between the ages of thirty to thirty-five are still unmarried. Nor is it only the men who escape matrimony so long. Forty-two per cent of all women who reach that age of middle life are single. In the United States, in England, in Denmark, in all other countries in fact, there is no such long delay in marrying. In all three of the coun-tries named, comparative figures for both men and women do not reach 25 per cent. Only in Ireland is a single man or woman of thirty the rule rather than the exception.

But it is not a question merely of the Irishman's hanging back a little longer from an inescapable fate. For a surprising number escape altogether. One man out of every four men who reach fifty in Ireland is still a bachelor. And though the women have slightly bet-ter luck in finding mates, the same figure holds for them.

Other countries usually delay marriage longest in the urban professional classes. But in Ireland, it is the country-people who marry latest. One can range the country in something of a scale in this regard. The more numerous in a county the numbers of small holdings, roughly, the later marriage takes place, and the greater number of bachelors, particularly males, of all ages, there are. Late marriage and bachelorhood are characteristics today of the countryman's way of life.

In the problem presented by these statistics, the structural approach to the countryman's way of life can bring a new illumination. It throws into relief the human setting in which economic and historical changes have run their course.

After the terrible disaster of the Famine, agriculture underwent a change. Canadian and Argentine wheat forced Irish land into cattle production. The great land clearances took place, turning out the population to make way for pasture. Then the small farmer followed the large into pasturage for dry cattle, on a lesser scale, and the milch cow declined. Small towns and crossroads distributing centres and the railroads sprang up all through the country; and abroad, the roaring industrial expansion, first of England and then of America, gave opportunities denied at home. Through all this: through curtailment of employment at home, through substitution of cattle for men upon the land, through denial of local opportunity, the stream of emigration kept its steady flow.

Through all this, too, the figures of Irish marriage kept pace. Age of marriage was normal in the year of the first census. In 1841 there was a normally low percentage of the unmarried in the population, and men and women married as early as they do in the United States today. At each decennial census afterwards, marriage was a little later and the unmarried a little more numerous. Through all the welter of changes, the figures grew steadily toward wider and wider spread celibacy.

Then when the economic and political tides turned, the human setting still endured. The clearances ceased; land reform won security of tenure; years of prosperity after 1870 brought an income that could be used more and more at home, as lowered rents spread and freehold was assured. Finally, the war brought undreamed-of prosperity and on its heels the strength for revolution and civil war. The milch cow came back to a position from which it had only retreated very little; dairying could be organized and come to vie with beef cattle as a market outlet. Finally, as a last step, industry began to make its call at home.

In all this flow of circumstance who can say what factor determined the numerical count of Irish population? Emigration went on as before, checked this year, hurried the next, until, perhaps from external check, the flow grew less and less.[1]

On the other hand, the corollary check on the population—late marriage—did not lag. It still grew. In the census of 1911 it reached its peak and has held it since. It alone shows no sign of falling-off in response to new economics and better days. For a social system is no brittle, changeable thing. Its adjustments to change and circumstance are a lesson, not in economics, but in the tenacity of human sentiment and human habit. Late marriage in Ireland can be associated with the reluctance of the old couple to renounce their leadership. It is part of the long struggle to acquire means to portion children. The closed corporation of the family cannot be dispersed until it is possible to establish a new one. The self-sufficiency of the group makes it always difficult to destroy. And now, today, the identification of a single family with a single individual farm prevents the setting up of more than one new group upon the land.

[1] Preliminary reports of the current (1936) census indicate emigration still continues, though now largely directed toward Great Britain rather than overseas.

So, when subdivision of holdings ceased after the Famine, Irish familism made its adaptation. The local community could not any longer settle its sons at home; it could no longer divide its land among them. Yet, unless it were to die it must live on. I say must, for a social system is co-extensive with the lives of its members. The Polynesians, in their island paradises, might die out nation by nation when their culture crashed, bled by a malady stronger than foreign germs or foreign guns. The Irish countrymen were tougher.

In living on, the system could still mould the lives of its members. As prosperity arrived, and land agitation fixed the attention of the farmer, 'land' became more and more a central value. Irish rural familism felt more and more strongly the threefold identification of 'land', 'blood' and local standing. Where land, alliance and prestige all follow the same lines, in marriage, the group finds its coherence in, and centres its tightly woven bonds round, that crucial reorganization of social life.

So, the 'landless' and the 'backward' must die out. In rural Ireland, however, it is not men but families which are so forced to their deaths. "Backward places do not grow big fortunes", we remember. That homely phrase is full of social meaning. The all-too-human drives for social rise, for prestige, leave them behind and marriageless. And in a familistic world, celibacy leads to extinction.

With the homely phrase we enter a new field in social life, yet one just as central to the way of rural Ireland. This is the broad area of social stratification. Under the awkward term are subsumed the judgments man makes among his fellows upon rank, upon prestige, upon inferiority and superiority, and the behaviours that embody them. All societies exhibit them; all organize them in one way or another. Even the ani-

mals show analogous behaviours. They practise domi-
nance and submit to subordination, though they cannot clothe their acts in words and build moralities and
philosophies out of them.

Today, in a democratic country, it is part of the
folkways either to deny that such activities exist, or
to demand that, like some unmentionable, they remain unstudied and unsaid. Yet, the student of human
behaviour cannot neglect so rich and so deep-rooted
a fount of human action. Nor can he afford to relegate
the study entirely to distant horizons. Caste in India is
a relatively safe topic for an American; caste in New
England or in the South is a high explosive. Only the
most painstaking objectivity and the most colourless
vocabulary can safeguard the temerarious investiga-
tor. And the only fair treatment is that of the laboratory: to treat the behaviours in their own settings and
to analyse them for nothing more than their function
in that setting. If one adopts this view, one can no
more blame the Smiths for snubbing the Joneses than
one can berate one protoplasm for repelling another.
In either case, one seeks the reason why and describes
the manner how.

In the Irish countryside we are dealing with
one broad class, the country-people. The behaviours
which preserve the distinctions between them and
others—townsmen, big farmers, gentry, and so on—do
not concern us here. Yet within their own community
—within the essential democracy of rural life—the
country-people can be seen to act in many ways to
separate, to draw distinctions, to repel the noncon-
formable. Remember that preposition 'within'. For
these behaviours do not discriminate between broad
groups, like the hauteur of a nobleman toward a
lackey.

They operate within a larger inclusion. They are

remotely like the ways of a schoolboy of the eighth grade who may scoff at the seventh-grader, look down on him, and bully him half in fun. Yet let the outside world break in, in the person of the teacher or rival schoolboys, and the distinction vanishes in the violence of united opposition. Nevertheless, intimate as they may be, these behaviours are none the less powerful. And like so much else in rural life, they find their chief expression and their most complete organization at the match, in country marriage.

From this fact springs the seeming paradox of Irish rural life. A social system centring so strongly round marriage and the family condemns a large proportion of its members to celibacy and long-preserved virginity. The explanation lies in the very paradox. Only the words are antithetical. It is through marriage that one's group and oneself attains and retains full stature. Failure in either sphere leaves unrealized the other.

From this fact, too, comes much of the homely comedy and tragedy of rural life. One prefers the human terms. That comedy and that tragedy show themselves to the student of social behaviour in another guise. They are controls upon the system. They are unconscious patterns of human action whose social function is to ensure conformities and to enforce cohesions against internal disruption and external defection. Much of the fate of human beings, both at their own hands and at those of their fellows, conforms to the controls the community exerts in response to the system of customs and values by which it builds itself and in which it ensures its preservation.

Tragedy, for example, lies in the fate of one romantic human type in rural Ireland. In the last century before the introduction of railroads and the growth of towns, each local community had its local artisans. Tailors, weavers, carpenters, shoemakers, smiths, followed their lifelong trades and supplied local needs. Open any account of rural Ireland before the last quarter of the last century, such as the tales of William Carleton, and you will be rewarded with a full-blooded picture of this lusty crew. Their crafts were very primitive, but their place was sure. Since then, nearly all of them, except the smith, their peer, have been swept away before the skill of townsmen and factory. These men supplied their neighbours, lived among them, were an integral part of rural life. When poverty struck too deep, they became peripatetics, like the wandering singers, scholars, fiddlers, spalpeen labourers, petty hawkers and beggars who swarmed the roads of Ireland. The world of fairy-tale was not remote from the farmers who knew these men. Rumpelstiltskin, in a Gaelic dress, was at one's very doors.

In remote communities some few of these survive. Where they do, the community can still make use of them. Commissioning them follows a traditional pattern of gifts and courtesies little resembling conventional monetary commerce. Their skill descends, like the farmer's farm, from father to son; it is 'in the blood'. Their surplus children must disperse to towns and in emigration. For theirs too is a familistic world.

Unless they marry within their own fast-diminishing numbers, they too must have land and fortune. Now and again one of them rises in the world. He acquires land, he sets aside a fortune, he marries sons and daughters on the land. Year by year, his trade goes into the discard, till one fine day he is a full-fledged small farmer.

But such upward mobility is rare and difficult. Economic change has swept his skill aside. The local artisan is more often a landless man, with nothing but a garden patch. The services he performs, however indispensable, do not give him equality with his neighbours. His standing is low, though his person is welcome. A farmer might 'put a son to a trade', perhaps, and often did not long ago. But it would be the lame son, the one not 'suited to the land'.

So today one finds broken remnants of this local craftsmanship scattered in cabins here and there through the countryside. The mere memory of their trade may be all that still remains to them to tell one that they are not the petty cotters they seem to be. They have not married, or if they have, without a fortune to transmit, they can find no wives and husbands for their children. Or here and there the countryman will point out the shells of their houses; "The family all died out of it", he will explain.

For the pressure of social standing is a powerful force, even in such a setting. Rather than admit an inevitable decline into the status of a landless labourer, they must 'die out of it'. One's standing, we remember, is one's blood. If they cannot amass a tangible representation of that blood in the dowry, they cannot marry. Neither alliance nor continuance can be theirs.

Even if they do succeed, and merge by marriage into the farmers' commonality, they bear a trace of a different origin yet a while longer. Change is slow where lines are tightly drawn; even peasant society knows its parvenus. And if dispute and anger flare up to strip life to its essential core, what insults do we hear? The countryman 'throws up' to his fellow, not his face or his manners or his animal likeness, in a wild *chameau* or *schwein*, but his descent. He damns him with the reminder of 'carpenter' or 'weaver blood'.

Strange as this epithet may seem to us, it brings an adequate, instantaneous response. The psychologist knows that expressions of anger, like any other emotion, are conditioned within particular social systems. And here the Irish system works, in its own fashion, to draw and to reinforce the inevitable distinctions and discriminations of social life.

From this fact springs comedy as well. Joke and fun play round this central theme. A good deal of old custom and traditional pastime cluster here. The picturesque buffoonery of the 'strawboys'—privileged masqueraded figures whose mock-dangerous invasion of the wedding feast has been dignified to represent a last remnant of a primeval bride-capture—is better explained thus more simply. Such symbolism as the gaiety of Shrove Tuesday, when in Clare, at least, young men beat loudly on the doors of those unmarried women who took no husband through the Shrovetide, is still direct enough.

For comedy and laughter soften the sharpness of social controls. They are the velvet glove that clothes the iron hand.

IV

Boys and Men

I have mentioned the rural community several times
throughout the previous lectures. Irish rural familism
is nothing if not bound to one's own stretch of countryside. But nowhere have I defined the term. I have
given you no adequate picture of the countryman's
way of life which ties it fast to time and place. I admit the deficiency. In self-justification I can only plead
my inability. A full-sized study of the human being
within a specific setting is not my art. It is that of the
novelist.

Yet the question of the organization of the community confronts the social anthropologist. He seeks to
analyse the means by which men relate themselves
over space and time. In Ireland, the question is important for the student of old custom, too. For tradition works locally.

Irish familism is of the soil. It operates most strongly
within allegiances to a definite small area. Life moves
within this area for the countryman; he very rarely
goes beyond it except on periodic visits to his market
town. He counts his fellows from within these same
narrow bounds. Beyond the next stream, over the next
hill, down the valley, a similar allegiance begins and
ends. Across the line are people no different from himself; but they are 'strangers', 'from beyond', or 'from
the other side'.

The countryman's round of life brings him into contact, close and intimate, with those within this area. The others in turn group themselves about him, through attachment to home and familiar associations. It is this group, defined variously in space, less so perhaps in numbers, that makes up the local community. However its topographic range may correspond to man-made or natural divisions of the earth's face, it is, first of all, a habit-woven social unity. Anyone who knows a summer resort has felt this fact. How little force the common landscape has in welding disparities, such as 'the summer people' and 'the natives'! Anyone who remembers childhood can recall the boundaries between his own gang and the next. For childish empires carve up space as quickly as do full-grown warrior bands.

To relate the form of the community, then, to rural life, once again leads to human behaviour. If I am to show you Irish familism in its proper local setting, I must bring you once more to observe and watch and question the life of the present. I do not mean the great antiquity of local groupings has no importance. Townland boundaries, parish lines, market areas, baronies, counties, dioceses and provinces often still to-day mark divisions among human beings that go back variously into remote past ages. A cleavage of the earth's face agreed upon long ago between forgotten clans can still persist in memory and influence conduct. The boundary of a parish, along which just the other day the countrymen fought hard-contested hurley-matches may once have marked an ancient kingdom's frontier. I mean, rather, that to understand the local past, one must first know the local present. Only then is it clear how such tradition moves and how it wields its force among men.

Therefore, I wish to devote this lecture to directing your attention inside such lines, to the behaviours which pattern local life inside them. We have already examined much of those that mark distinctions within the community, dividing it by 'blood' and by prestige. A good deal more could well be said of kinship and social stratification, were it not that we must hurry on. The existence of similar patterns which redirect integration across such distinctions is a new challenge.

One such pattern thrusts itself into notice immediately and insistently in rural Ireland. It clusters about age and age status. The conducts and sentiments round age are perhaps the most important factor, after familism, in shaping the countryman's way of life. Naturally, they are related to all that I have described before; they dovetail into family life. In them, the community finds its most compatible and its most enduring organization. No other social disposition sets a deeper stamp upon the countryman. No other is more immediate to the observer, tourist or anthropologist. No other, too, explains better why old custom lives today.

Ireland is in many ways an old person's country. Where emigration carries youth away, old age is disproportionately numerous. But that fact is not all the story, for the rural Irish are long-lived. The country districts set a norm for the Free State which shows itself statistically. Despite poverty, hardship, and the erroneously assumed 'decline of rural life', the countryman lives long and dies, often very old indeed. Many causes have been sought for this strange fact, but might it not be after all a simple matter? They live long because they have much to live for. In their own sphere of life, they are honoured; they have power.

We remember that the household and the family centres itself in them. Their room is semi-sacred in the fairy-lore; it is the best in the house. The chair by the fire, the seat of honour and most comfort, is theirs. Even with the transfer of command up on the farm, they are objects of marked deference.

But this is more than a family matter. The old people have privilege among and receive respect from others than their own relatives. The conduct which bestows both upon them is as much the folk custom of the community as it is the habit of family life. Where necessary, the community can enforce its maintenance. The community can, as it were, invade the family and regulate its members through gossip, verbal censure, and more rarely, direct intervention in the person of the priest.

The countryman's vocabulary is full of allusions to values upon age. A great deal of the judgments and the comments he makes upon his surroundings express them. Naturally, they do not discuss the organization of behaviour upon age in explicit terms; for such conducts are 'natural' and unchangeable in the minds of those who are shaped by them. But they are never silent upon the implications of such organization as it affects individual conduct in daily life. The upstart 'boy', the 'bold' child, the 'old man who ought to have shame for acting like that' are as constant objects of reproof and censure as the 'bad' father or son.

In general statements, one hears many expressions, day after day, which arise from the speaker's place within an age group. The broad opposition between 'old' and 'young' colours rural thinking powerfully. A great deal of the constant talk which flows back and forth among the 'friends' and neighbours who pass their lives within the rural community takes its form within this social context.

This is particularly true of discussion of the past. The past is a favourite topic; the 'old days' something of an obsession in the countryside. This is not only because one of the listeners was the anthropologist 'looking for old custom'. For, where descent is a critical nexus of habitual relationship and old age the most honoured state, the past cannot fail to be the focus of interest.

Thus the older men and women are very partial to the things of their own age. And the young people are, in part, swept along with them. The 'old times' are a very ready topic among the country-people. Many a time an old person will be got to tell of them; he or she takes little warming to the task. They were the hard times, even bad times, of famine and death but the speakers throw a glow of courage and glamour round them. There were few tools, no draft-animals, no shoes, none of the amenities of present existence. The listeners murmur phrases of commiseration and shake their heads in pity. "Weren't they the bad old times?" and "Wasn't it hard the work they had to do in the old days?" they ask one another. But there is a tinge of pride in their voices, in the manner of tellers and listeners alike.

For remembered necessities, in the eyes of the old people who tell the tale, are now feats of endurance to which the new generation could never aspire. That is the point for those who tell and those who listen. Where could you get a young man today to walk from Corofin to Ballinasloe, walk in his bare feet the forty miles and back over the stony roads? Where is the woman today who could shoulder a creel of turf a hundred yards out through the bog mud to the famine road, before the Board put in the road to the bog above Dunnagore?

Often the expressions take a different turn. They become that universal complaint—the younger generation. "Young people aren't what they used to be," said one old farmer in the course of a general discussion of the golden age that was his youth. "They spend money for fags, they have to be gambling every night, or else to a dance, and if they happen to win a turkey they will nearly shake the house down [in their triumph]. There is no good in the country when things go on like this. In the old days a man used always be out repairing his stone walls, cleaning his land, or doing something. Now you can't get them to do anything unless you pay them."

Here he paused for an illustration, chose one from among his own cronies, and swept volubly on. "Wasn't old Keane out every night with his cattle and he putting them in small fields and late in the night? Wasn't he up early in the morning and out working? They cleared a nice piece of land in the common. He kept at it till he had cattle all the way up by Ballyvaughan. You wouldn't get any of the young people to do that now. There's no controlling them."

Discussions of the present fall into the same vein. The past, for the older members of the community, reflects their glories and serves as a convenient vehicle for the expression of their superiority. In the same spirit, the present can be measured against the past, usually only to be found lacking.

But these statements express much more than a mere rivalry between old and young. They spring from a mutuality between them which transcends rivalry. The old days are better among other things, because the interdependence of young and old was greater. The present is less attractive because the old no longer control the young, and the young no longer aid the old, as they should. Both facts of this interrelation may be expressed, even though the speaker, if he be old, may cast them in terms of mistrust and dislike for the young. In fact, the whole of experience may be brought within this scheme of attitudes. To give an example, here is one old fellow's rationalization of his misgivings about the present Irish school system:

"I am patriotic and it may be a bad thing to say but I think the school system they have now is bad and the teaching of Irish is bad. In my day and before, a man might go to school when he could—maybe for only three months in the year. But he would know more than they get now when they go to school all the time. The old people learned more then. When a child finished school he would be expected to read a newspaper to the old people, and to write a letter for them, or to do sums. And he would do it well." His complaint is much longer but you have heard enough to see his mistrust of a system which to his mind makes no provision for the mutuality between young and old.

This mutuality was and is strongest in the realm of farm work. The farm family demands the co-operation of all its members. No less the community makes its valuation of young and old upon that co-operation. General discussions among the country-people bring out this fact again and again. To illustrate by quotation once more: two old fellows, adult farmers with families, could reach agreement upon a formula running somewhat as follows:

"The men were stronger in the past, they worked harder, while you try to get any young person to do as much work as the old men now and they would laugh at you. The young people today seem to see how little work they can do rather than how much. While the old men would strip down and compete with one another to see who can do the most work."

So they went on, but even in the midst of their theme they were forced to admit that there were compensations: "It is true for you that the people in the old times weren't as knacky as they are now. Wasn't it how they used to have the horse in a stall feeding, while they [themselves] would be out with a spade turning over the garden [and no plough]."

Most of these allusions are to the realm of farm work. Just as the rivalry between father and son is most intimate and most constant in the economy which they pursue together, so the expression of the conflict between the generations in the community takes the same form.

You will probably ask if there are not grains of truth in the older generation's statements. My answer is that I neither know nor care. And I feel the countryman is not much more concerned. For this is a very old rivalry and once its expression was even more formalized than it is today. We owe the first poem of the eighteenth-century poet O'Rahilly to the expression of this rivalry, in an older day when Gaelic poetry still survived. He was called in to defend the young unmarried men, the 'boys' of today, in a poetic contest over respective merits between them and the 'old men', that is, the married men of family and substance. And he played, too, in the hurley game which fought out the contest in another field. For we are dealing here not so much with truths or falsities as with group-attitudes reciprocally held. Pareto would call them derivations; he would find their residues in the sentiments of those grouped together about a common status in the community. Once these sentiments were expressed ceremonially as in O'Rahilly's day. Even now the men of Luogh point out a large stone. With that stone the 'men' and the 'boys' competed at tests of strength till just a few years ago.

For the young people do not agree with their elders on the score of their own shortcomings. They do not express these attitudes. They have a good deal to say, on the other hand, among themselves from their own point of vantage. They express the reverse of the medal. The past is not so golden to them; and there are many among their elders whose idiosyncrasies can be swept aside with some such sweeping condemnation as 'old fool' and 'old blatherer'. Like the son I quoted in the last lecture, who listened patiently to his father, only to follow his own devices, they have their own valuations in which youth and strength outweigh age and ripe experience.

Yet within a system of values in which the old represent the nexus of kinship and bear honour within the community, the young people do not see the issue so clearly. There is as much respect as there is antagonism in their verbal assessment of the old people. In the non-verbal behaviour of daily conduct, deference is uppermost. This fact sobers their group's egocentricity. In their position there is a necessary balance between subordination and compensatory vauntings and distastes. If you remember Synge's *Playboy*, you remember how reality broke in upon the playboy when the community saw his father still very much alive.

So, within this framework the young men can recognize themselves as a distinct group—an age grade, to use technical language. They have their own interests and sentiments, opposed in the scheme of rural life to those of their elders. Various places, pursuits and forms of activity are their own preserve. They greet the suggestion that they should take their place in the gatherings of the old men with something of the derision they reserve for women. But the ambivalence of their attitudes makes general expression difficult. Their position imposes silence, except among themselves. Consequently, one finds their attitudes rather more frequently in particular annoyances, boredoms and chafings against restraint. Rural ceremony gives them few outlets today; the fine articulateness of O'Rahilly's day is either dammed or searches out more devious outlets.

The sentiments of both groups, then, are the products of a system of values about age status. The individual makes his statements and entertains his feelings by virtue of the place he occupies. These express not only a rough grouping of individuals of similar age and status but a rough interrelation between the groups so composed. They form a scaffolding of categorization in which each person takes his relative place.

One can trace this process in rural Ireland in the many names and epithets the local community bestows. Local titles are ephemeral; they have little currency outside the immediate circle of the townland and the village. At best they spread through a parish. They are nicknames, and express no more than the named-one's place in the hearts of his fellows. Yet many of them, too, are generic epithets and like 'old' and 'young' they may prefix a name and designate the bearer's social place. They thus come to express broad categories of a man's behaviour and describe not a biological or a physiognomic but a sociological individuality. All well-developed social systems show this power; rural Ireland makes much use of it.

Thus two common epithets in the brogue are of this latter kind. The countryman speaks often of a 'saint', in praise, and a *cailleach*, in condemnation. Both words refer only to the 'old'. In strict linguistics, both are metaphors, of course, for the brogue knows and makes use of the words in their proper meanings. *Cailleach*, the Gaelic word, is properly a 'hag' or 'witch'. A 'saint', of course, is canonized by the Church.

But the countryman who refers to this or that contemporary as a *cailleach* or a saint is not concerned with purity of diction. He is making a sociological categorization with an ethical bias. He is judging an old man or woman for his or her success in filling the role rural life assigns. His thinking is social, not reformist, as the term has come to be loosely used, but rather conditioned within the dispositions of a particular social pattern. Thus one man in Luogh, already referred to, who was a model of family harmony and 'had a kind word for everyone' in the local community, was a 'saint'. Another old fellow, a leader in his village, could be described by a neighbour as follows:

"That old man is a typical Irishman. He is a saint and there isn't a thought against anyone in him. He is always in a good humour and if he went to town to take a drink he could stand in the one place till he dropped. He is as harmless as a child. He and his friend Roche are two level-headed farmers and they have met every sort of trouble. If you are in doubt about any advice in farming, you can go to them and they will give as good advice as you can get. It would pay a young man to listen to them."

I have quoted this rural eulogy for a reason. It shows much better than words of mine could how the speaker's mind could flow uninterruptedly, without any sense of transition, from ethical judgment to agricultural advice. For 'saintliness' of this kind is a matter of filling a social role. But it is one's role for the community that counts. That role runs all the way from peaceful and friendly demeanour to directing farm work. There is nothing individual in it; it is the behaviour the community patterns about the old man. It is his *noblesse oblige*. That the word 'saint' should be borrowed from religion should surprise no one. It is merely proof that one society survives in western civilization in which theology and the popular mind have not yet suffered a divorce. The early Puritan and the ancient Roman would have understood such a state of affairs.

Relative age thus makes a difference in status in the local community. It fits one into a definite place in a scheme of values, and lastly, it equips one with a definite role in communal life which one can fill well or ill.

The conduct that reflects this state of affairs thrusts itself into the observer's view again and again in rural Ireland. One finds it wherever one meets the countrymen together. The relations between young and old in the community, like those between parent and child within the family, are understandable in the light of the roles of the broad age groups.

First, there is the matter of privilege and precedence. To an outsider there may seem little enough in the countryman's way of life to allow for such distinctions. But from within, that little looms much greater. The old fellows, the men of full status who head farms and farm-working corporations of sons— those who have turned or are about to turn over their control to a younger generation—are accorded a very real precedence. In their own houses we have seen it to be very great; in the community at large it is little less so. A farmer visiting another takes his place at the hearth seat, his sons lag behind and occupy the back of the room. When the community gathers in the wake-house to honour the dead, the places by the fire go to the old adult 'men' and 'women'; the 'boys and girls' must group themselves behind. They come forward only when called upon. At country 'stations' the elder men and women file in for confession and come forward for communion first. On the road to shop, church or fair, the young man must keep pace, and the elder may call him to his side.

The relation shows itself best perhaps in the constant discussions that are the breath of life for the countryman. No work is too pressing to prevent the countryman from 'stopping on the road to pass the time of day'. In the rural community such personal communion is an indispensable bridge across the social and physical space separating farm from farm. In all such discussion it is the elder men who may regulate length and subject of conversation. When groups form, in pubs, in one another's houses on evening visits, before and after mass in the churchyard, the enthralling game of presenting argument, choosing sides, directing the flow of talk, belongs to the older men. The young men must 'listen in'.

At such times the important news of the countryside disseminates itself. Political judgments are formed, and the ephemeral decisions of daily life are made. In all this the 'boys' are silent listeners. It is a bold young man who enters an opinion of his own.

Then, secondly, there is the matter of the contacts of the community with the outside world. The elder men, these same father-owners, represent the interests of the community, before priest, schoolmaster, merchant, cattleman and government official. The younger men hang back, ready to be brought in when the elders want them, listening in and keeping their own counsel.

The relation extends in fact to very small matters indeed. The better cup of tea, the bigger piece of bread, the two eggs instead of one, the pipeful of tobacco, go to the older men. This last, tobacco, is no small matter where even now tobacco is still expensive enough to require careful husbanding. It is a custom in the country districts to pass the pipe round among one's intimates and guests, for testing, for praise, and to the accompaniment of formulae still often magical in nature. But the pipe does not go to the young man; he must content himself with an occasional 'fag'. When there is little, the young man can go without.

For illustration there is the anecdote that one Clare farmer tells: "During the time when tobacco was scarce [the war], an old man came into Sullivan's [shop] and asked for a half-quarter [cut of tobacco]. The Missus told him to go [get it] where he always bought it. He was very cast down. After he was out the door I said to her—she should give him some tobacco because a man who is used to it all his life would miss it greatly if he can't get it. Let the young bucks go, says I, they don't want it. But an old fellow wants it badly. She looked at me and says, Frank, are you serious? I am, faith, says I; call back the old man. He was just a few paces down the road. She did, and his face lighted up and he couldn't thank her enough."

Informal as these differences are, they are nevertheless powerful agents in the regulation of conduct among small farmers. Without them the flavour of rural life is lost. Without them, too, one can gain no understanding of the continual round of informal activities of social intercourse which fill the non-working lives of the countrymen. For the country-people have their entertainments, like their more sophisticated urban contemporaries. The student of society cannot afford to dismiss them as inconsequential. They are often important controls of human activity.

When my colleagues and I first made our way into the rural communities we were to come to know best, we were plunged into a mass of observations which seemed to have no interpretation. Night after night, their day's work done, our new acquaintances, at least the males among them, walked out upon the roads to this house and that in search of recreation and companionship. Mention of dances, gambles, sings, *cei-*

lidhthe, filled our ears, belying the impression of a
grey monotony of rural life too easily gathered by
town-bred minds. Some of these sportive gatherings
were age-old customs like the bonfires of St. John's
Eve; others celebrated crucial events, such as wakes,
christenings, weddings. But many others were less occasional and less specialized gatherings; and others
again wore a very modern dress: a turkey raffle and
a dance round a gramophone.

But our interest was soon caught by distinctions of
participation, rather than those of kind. The personalities of the 'village' participated variously, different
groups met more or less regularly at specific houses.

For instance, the 'old fellows' went out on *cuaird,*
as they called their visiting, to join one another. They
followed a deep-set regular habit. As they phrased it
"a man would feel lonely if he didn't go out on *cuaird*".

In most communities they usually convened at a
particular house. Often their gatherings bore particular names. In one North Clare community, Rynamona
by name, the old men's meeting was known as the
'Dáil'. Before the Free State, it had been the 'parliament'. The name is a jocular one, of course, but as we
shall see, it is expressive of the participants' evaluation of themselves, none the less.

The young men know the 'Dáil' as the 'old men's
house'; they stay away. One of the cronies of Rynamona put the matter most clearly, when he described
the old men's gathering from its members' point of
view:

"It wouldn't suit [for the young men to come]," he
said. "They gather in at Jack Roche's and they laugh
and joke and play cards; they talk about the next
gamble and the next dance, and that is all they know.
It is a lot of codology [he means, nonsense, bun-
combe]. It is only the old men, the men with families

and a responsibility on them, they are the ones that come. And in our own way we learn a great deal. If you advance any argument you must be prepared to defend it from all attack, and John Roche, 'the public prosecutor', will ask you questions till he is sure it is right or wrong. Then some evening we have real discussions in which we settle problems. Other times we discuss farming. It wouldn't suit for the young men to come in, but when we get old and they get married, then they will gather just as we do and talk about this and that. That is the way it always has been and that is the way it always will be. There is never any bad blood between any of the village, and one reason is because we talk things over."

The statement, then, imparts a deeper reality to what appears at first sight to be merely a companionable pastime of the older men. This meeting of theirs is a clique, a tightly knit group of males of similar status and interests. It is strong enough and binding enough to bestow nicknames upon its members as in the case of the 'public prosecutor'. But it is a clique, too, which operates within a traditional setting. It has a function to perform for others than the cronies who make it up. The speaker claims for it at least that it prevented bad blood in the village.

In such a clique, the student of social behaviour can see fairly closely the interplay of social dispositions and individual character. Concrete cases have a way of disposing of controversies by transporting the issue to a new plane. In the study of such a case as this, as we shall see, the old question whether the individual affects the society or the society moulds the individual—a long-standing scholastic debate among sociologists—can be pushed into well-merited oblivion. For the answer is that both interpretations are correct; and that neither is at all penetrating. The

issue is free to move to a new plane: the relations between behaviours and the patterning of sentiment
and conduct.

In the old men's clique of Rynamona we have our
concrete instance. Similar old men's gatherings from
any other of the rural communities my colleagues and
I knew would serve as well. They are remarkably similar even to duplicating nicknames. For as our in-
formant explains: "That is the way it always was and
that is the way it always will be". A social system
endures in past and future and exists in space, its
changes are changes of this spatial and temporal
world, its constancies are likewise bound to earth and
time.

Rynamona, then, shall be our present instant in
time and space. Rynamona is a medium-sized townland in the limestone country of North Clare. It is like
many another of the 'good land' of rough limestone
outcrops that stretch back from the sea into the gla-
ciated lake-stream North Clare country. To reach
Rynamona is no easy task, even for horse and car. The
main road north out of Corofin to Kilfenora passes
through Killinaboy, where twelve houses, a school, a
chapel and a post-office mark an ancient settlement.
Only a ruined ninth-century church and graveyard
attest to its great antiquity.

There, beside the graveyard, a side-road leads off
toward Glanquin mountain, and the hills of Burren
beyond. One follows this road along through ragged
upland for a mile and a half. This is Killinaboy Com-
mons, and its many small fields, laboriously cleared
of stones, bear witness to its having been a refuge of
the evicted. The upland is not high. It merely gives
rise enough to start a half-mile of gentle slope into a
basin whose bottom is filled with a little lake. Ryna-

mona lies round the lake, at the end of a rough borheen.

The fields here are cleared, too, and cut up between
with limestone ridges. Yet the grass grows richly among
the crags, and the farmers are a fairly prosperous lot.

Eight of their houses stand in an irregular cluster
on the lake shore. This is 'Rynamona village'. Five
others are scattered through the fields and across the
lake. These households, with a few more a little far-
ther off, make up the community.

The farms are all small; they are of the kind we
have met in Luogh. None has ten cows, and only one
has a single beast. Except for the eight houses hud-
dled in the village, fields and meadows stretch away
from the haggard wall. In the case of the villagers, the
fields are scattered about and behind the haggards in
irregular patterns. Besides these home fields, most of
Rynamona has two or three acres in additions carved
out for them by the Land Commission on an estate
about two miles off.

Rynamona is a closely knit community. Redupli-
cated bonds of kinship unite all the households. "We
are all related one way or another", they say. 'Cooring'
is the usual form of co-operation. The village holds
itself responsible amid grumbles for maintaining the
borheen which leads out to the outside world of the
towns. Nowadays, the County Council pays the sons
who break stones and lay them in the winter months,
but the village still assigns a bit of the road to each
householder. Small matter if the borheen is bad, for a
well-trod maze of paths criss-crosses the fields in all
directions.

Old man O'Donoghue's house, the third in the village, is the 'old men's house'. Mrs. Ruin, a neighbour,
will tell you what the old man means to the men of
the village. "The old man is getting weaker and when

he is gone out of it the village won't be the same. He will be the greatest loss. It is round his fireplace the men gather. Where will they go when he dies?"

But the question has not yet arisen for the men who meet there nearly every night, particularly in winter, when the evening is long and the day's work shortest. Soon after supper they begin to gather. Perhaps this or that *habitué* may not come, but it is always the same group of men who stride across the threshold with a "God bless all here" and take their accustomed places.

O'Donoghue has the place of honour. He sits in the chair to the right of the fire. He is an old man now and no longer very active beyond the house door. He lives here with his nephew, a man of fifty, and his wife. The nephew and nephew's wife have no children, but must depend upon their own efforts in the working of the farm. It is a good farm; the nephew works it well, deferring to the old man's judgment in most matters.

O'Donoghue is the 'judge' in this gathering. In the nightly discussions which take place round his hearth he has a judicial role. He is regarded as a wise man. All must defer to his opinions. Usually he contents himself with a word of affirmation, or now and again, a slow, measured judgment upon a current topic. He initiates nothing. Only occasionally does he add a non-judicial bit to the conversation. Then he shows himself to have a fund of funny and apt anecdote as good as any other man's. He rarely generalizes; when he does, his theme is the 'old times'.

Silent as this shrewd old man is, his is the central position in the group. Comments and questions are phrased through him. He takes the proffered verbal bit and passes it on among the others. And, when agreement is finally reached, it is his quiet "so it is" that settles the point for good.

O'Halloran sits on the hob across the hearth from him. He is the 'drawer down' in the scheme of jocular titles which includes most of the group. O'Halloran is a mature man of fifty or more. He owns a farm a little better perhaps than most, just beyond the village. He works it with his wife and six children, the eldest of whom is nearly thirty. As he has no parents left alive, O'Halloran is the 'old man' and the 'man of the house'. But, individually, he is more. "He has a great head on him", they say. He has had a somewhat wider experience; once he travelled over the roads of southern Ireland as a salesman. Yet, though he is a little sceptical occasionally, and his politics are somewhat suspect to the villagers, who are de Valera men today, almost to a man, he is emphatically one of them.

His title of 'drawer down' is an apt one. O'Halloran seeks information. Most frequently it is he who brings up points of interest and questions of the day. These he addresses to O'Donoghue, who passes them on for general discussion. Like all the rest of them, he is most at home in finding apt illustrations in definite, precisely told anecdotes. But his chief role is to 'draw the talk down' to common levels of interest.

O'Loughlin usually occupies the other hob. He has no real place here. He is a bachelor, aged fifty or more, and though he comes here, he has little to say. He is silent nearly all the time. When he breaks silence it is only to add to unanimity. For O'Loughlin, the bachelor, lives alone, is very poor, and having no family, can neither 'coor' nor work his land to best advantage. Occasionally he works with the 'boys' at stone-breaking on the roads. Just as he has no voice here, he has no title either.

Roche, the 'public prosecutor', sits in the chair be-

fore the hearth opposite the old man O'Donoghue.
He is a man of sixty. He has a wife and an unmarried
son and daughter, both in their thirties, still at home.
His is a good farm, and he is still active upon it.
Roche also has a reputation for shrewdness, but his
role here is a different one. Roche demands 'why', he
forces one to parade one's best arguments, he pursues
a point relentlessly to its final conclusion. There his
interest stops, and he makes way for O'Donoghue,
who sums up the agreement of the group.

Roche earns his title well; he tests one's mettle. No
one takes offence at his 'prosecution'. It clears the issue and brings out the right and the wrong upon
which all can agree and O'Donoghue phrase judgment.

Behind these two, a little further into the middle of
the room, sits Cullinan, the 'senator'. Cullinan lives
across the lake. He works a middling farm with his
wife and five children. Several of the sons are nearing
twenty-five, and Cullinan himself is well past fifty.

The 'senator' is a 'weighty' man. His part here is in
character. Cullinan is the one of them most fertile in
cogent and fitting anecdotal illustration. In a scheme,
such as this, of reference to past event and traditional
precedent, Cullinan's memory of persons and happen-
ings, slowly and accurately, even pompously phrased,
gives 'weight' to the evening's discussions.

Still further behind them, and often perched upon
settle or table in this kitchen, are two other *habitués*.
The elder of them is Ruin, a man of sixty, who lives
in the village with a wife considerably younger than
himself, and two boys and a girl, out of a once more
numerous progeny, still at home. The children are in
their twenties, and help him in his still active conduct
of the farm.

Privately, at least, the others think Ruin 'a bit of a

fool'. He is as good a farmer as any of them, it is true, and knows how to drive a shrewd bargain. But his role at *cuaird* is not a weighty one. Ruin is a very voluble man; he can be counted upon at all times to enliven the gathering with a deal of opinion upon all subjects. His volubility makes him more vulnerable than the rest to the 'public prosecutor's' relentless logic. Nevertheless, it helps to keep the conversation alive and active. Consequently, though he has no important title, Ruin is a member of long standing.

The younger of the two men sitting in back, of which Ruin is one, is John Quinn. His position is a little anomalous, though he is a Rynamona man by birth and blood. Quinn works a good farm just beyond the village. He married-in there, taking over the place of a dead husband. But, true to country custom, it was not the widow he married. She brought in a sister who in turn married Quinn. Both women are still living in the house. But the elder sister has become the 'old woman' and is treated more like a parent than like a contemporary. It is Quinn and his wife who work the farm and regard it as their own. Their claim would be a perfect one, were it not for one misfortune; they are childless, at fifty.

Quinn is thus neither fully a young man nor fully an old one, as the countryside reckons age status. And his place in the evening gathering reflects this indeterminate state. In the two years in which my colleagues and I had Rynamona under observation, Quinn was going through a transition. It was one which he could not describe himself, but one which showed itself well in his behaviour.

When we first came, Quinn divided his evenings between the old men's house and card-playing in several of the young men's gathering places. At one of these, he was an important figure. His pronouncements were listened to with respect. He had 'weight'. He showed in his serious manner a little disdain for frivolous pursuits.

In the old men's house, however, he looked a different figure. He was often silent, or contented himself with answering questions. When he did speak, it was to 'act the playboy', in the country phrase. It seemed to be a periodic fluctuation with him. One evening he would be silent, and the next he would be more than ready to joke, to render a song, to break into playful banter. Sometimes his efforts were successful, sometimes they were not.

But Quinn's playboy role did not last long. A year later he was an *habitué* of the old men's *cuaird*; he had given up all other visits. He had moved in. O'Donoghue, 'the judge', passed judgment one evening which affirmed his new place. "He's a bit of a playboy", he said, "but he has a good head on him."

These seven men make up the old men's *cuaird*. One can see how closely knit a clique they are. They have code and values of their own, strong enough to enforce specific personalities on each of the members, in accordance with the role of each in the group.

But there is an external side to this clique as well. To appraise the *raison d'être* of such a group in Rynamona, one must know its place in the community. These seven men, for instance, are not the only old men in Rynamona. Roche the 'public prosecutor' has a brother, with a good farm, across the line between Rynamona and the next townland, Carhunamadra. But the elder Roche is seventy-five and no longer stirs out the door; he is too feeble. His sons, still 'young men', work the farm.

But there is also another, and more active, old fellow. Moroney is, perhaps, the 'strongest' farmer in Rynamona. His house in the village is the best in the townland, and his farm the best stocked. Moroney and his wife, at sixty, work it with the help of a son and daughter, both nearing thirty. Each year, Moroney stands for them all at the 'station' and the family's dues to the Church are greater than any other's in Rynamona. Such prosperity draws Moroney a bit apart from the villagers. Occasionally, in discussions of politics, he will identify himself with the Cosgrave party, as a man with a 'stake in the country'.

All this sets Moroney a bit apart. Some say there was an incident long ago when Moroney was young; but most have forgotten it. Nevertheless, the breach is there. Moroney never attends at the old men's house.

Furthermore, just as not all the old men of Rynamona come to O'Donoghue's, so are there also households which have no representative there. With them, however, the transition we saw in John Quinn's case has scarcely begun. Two examples will show you the case. O'Brien is a man of forty. He is married, his parents are dead, his children none older than fifteen. He is eligible in age and status, perhaps, but he does nothing to hasten the transition from young man to old. For O'Brien is a man of moody temper, given to gusts of anger. He goes out very little at all; when he does it is to the young men's gambles.

With Mackey, the process is hardly begun. Mackey's parents are dead, and the farm is his. But Mackey is only very recently married, and he sent off a brother to the towns only a year or so ago. He, too, still visits with the young men.

Therefore, with these easily accounted-for exceptions, the old men's house includes all the farm-fathers of complete families. It is made up of those who are married and in the words already quoted 'have a responsibility on them'. Informal as it is, it nevertheless unites these men of full status within the community and unites them, too, in such a way as to crystallize and canalize the influence their status gives them.

For this clique is built round discussion and decision, as its nicknames show us, because discussion and decision are its role for the community at large. In the persons of these old men, in their deliberation, the integration of the community is accomplished.

The old man's superior status in the family and in the community cannot be separated from his half of a mutuality which unites him to his subordinates, and gives him, as it were, his *noblesse oblige*. In the same way, the old men's clique operates.

For here in the old men's house, the countryman's way of life exerts its strongest sway upon him. It is the 'parliament' of his fellows. The topics brought up and debated upon are much the same from year to year and place to place. Agriculture, perhaps, comes first. Times of sowing, reaping and harvesting are debated. Prices are compared, innovations tested. Traditional methods receive their strongest support here, in the web of legend, proverb and reference to the past the speakers throw round them.

Much of the community's relation to the outer world takes its form here, determined in the old men's argument and agreement. In late years this has come to be called 'politics'. Petitions for relief road work, for expansion of agricultural prize schemes, most, in fact, of the business of the County Council and its committees originates on the side of local community in the discussions of the old men's *cuaird*. It is here, too, that the community reaches unanimity in party voting. In Rynamona, for instance, it is felt that the interest of all demands that there should be no dissension on the score of politics. Consequently, even O'Halloran, the 'drawer down', whose private views leaned in a different direction from those of the villagers, begged that no word of his heterodoxy be allowed to reach the ears of Rynamona. "I wouldn't want them to think I wasn't with them", he put it. No wonder, then, that the political allegiances of whole countrysides are constant factors in Irish politics.

The community reaches agreement upon its internal affairs, too, through the old men's discussions. It is in just this type of activity that one can at last put one's finger upon that nebulous force among men: public opinion. That force is not implemented; it is merely the power of gossip and censure; only in critical days, as in the time of land agitation, can it rise to action, as a last resort, and win itself an international name: the boycott. But it is none the less powerful.

But, in rural Ireland, the group through which this power flows serves another function which cannot be disassociated from its role as the seat of public opinion. The members of the old men's *cuaird* are the living repositories of tradition. In communities, such as Luogh, where the Irish language lingers on, many of them are *seana-chaidhthe* or story-tellers. Among them the ancient repertories of legend, saga and folk-tale still find an audience. That the exponents of fairy-lore have always been, and are still, old men and old women, is no social accident. For the pattern of local life retains its continuity and preserves what it can of its conformity with the past through them.

But what of the young men, those who have not attained full status? They do not attend at the old men's house; they take no part in the deliberations there. From their own point of vantage, they scorn their elders, as much as their subordinate position allows. And they, too, walk out on *cuaird* upon the roads night after night and gather-in at this house and that.

In Rynamona, they were as ardent evening visitors as the older men. But their habit showed a great difference. There was no single central clique so closely knit as that of the old men's house. They had no larger justification, as the old men had, for their meetings. They went because, frankly, "you never feel the time passing when you're in with the boys". They formed pairs of lads, brothers, friends, and groups of three and four and five who habitually played cards or walked the roads together. A still greater difference marked these groups. One rarely heard them talk of the affairs of the community. There was no debate, no reaching of decisions, no appeal to tradition and precedent. They spoke most often of their own plans, and the trials of their own age and kind. The skills upon which the cliques prided themselves and from which they drew their nicknames were of other sorts. Not even farming occupied a large share of their conversation, keen as their rivalry often was when work was going on.

In Rynamona the most frequent centre for the gatherings of the young men was the house of Roche, 'the public prosecutor', whose eldest son, a keen farmer about thirty, was something of a leader among them. Most of the young men between twenty-five and thirty-five met there. Through the winter months they met nearly every night, and played the usual games of the countryside, 'nap' and 'forty-five', often far into the wee hours. Other groups through the community met like these men and followed like pursuits with an equal zest.

At times, a custom somewhat more organized, the 'gamble', unites them all. It often brings in other young men across the lines separating community from community. As often as once a week, a gamble is held in or near Rynamona. Each household in its turn throws open its doors to the card-players. Admission, usually a shilling, goes to defraying the expense of a supper and tea for all and goes toward the prize.

For the gamble is one of many sporting events. The prize may be a turkey, or two geese, even a young pig or calf. Elaborate conventions govern the play, and the winner may count himself a proud man. To be known in the countryside, far and wide, as a 'great gambler' is a coveted distinction proving shrewdness and skill. The country dance is another such event, and still enlivens the countryside in the winter months, bringing the younger members of the communities together and providing honour for the distinguished. For 'a great dancer' is as widely known. In summer, hurley, the national game, has the same effect; and nowadays, through the nation-wide organization of the Gaelic Athletic Association, the 'great hurler' may win his way to the admiration of all Ireland.

But at home, in the local community, the young men remain what they are. Their distinction lifts them not at all from their status. Their skills are nothing more than proficiencies. The pursuits of the subordinate generation are no more than 'good times' that 'pass the time'. For, through no plan or design, but merely through the force of the social organization of values and behaviours, the activities of the young men's cliques exert no larger role within the community.

For the young men's cliques do not primarily serve to knit the community as a whole the more firmly. The difference is structural. The activities of the young men unite them from farm to farm, from clique to clique, even from one community to the next. The integration of the young men is a looser and less inclusive integration than that the old men's clique performs, even though the numbers ephemerally joined in gamble, dance or hurley match are much greater.

For the old men's clique unites, in its controlling voice, both young and old. The old men's clique unites the old men in terms of their common individual positions as recipients of the respect of the community, and as heads, owners and commanders of their family corporations. It expresses for the community the same subordination of the young men that is their lot within their families.

In such a case, the course of the countryman's path through rural life is plainly charted. In the normal event, the circle of his friends and contemporaries must change and progress. There comes a time when either he or they must break away altogether. Distinction in the world of the young men's pursuits is at best but a nine days' or nine years' wonder. He faces perforce a new orientation of sentiment and a new sort of behaviour. Just as he moves to a new social place at marriage, he must move onward among the cliques of his fellows in the community.

The case of John Quinn in Rynamona, the new-comer to the old men's house, can bear re-examination in this light. Quinn first belonged to a group which met at the house of one Joseph McMahon, better known as Oscair, the Hercules of Irish saga, for his great strength. Oscair was the centre of the group. He was a rural carpenter, with only a small plot of garden and his house. But he was a good workman, a good singer, a gay-hearted jokester, and something of a repository of folk-tale. He was between forty-five and fifty.

The men who collected round Oscair's fire were aged from thirty-five to sixty. Like their age, their habit was intermediate between old and young. Talk was the order of the day; they seldom played cards. Oscair's song and ballad enlivened the gathering.

Some of the men who came here spoke with 'weight'; they tried to turn the talk into a discussion of the affairs of the community. Old Moroney, the 'strongest' farmer of Rynamona, who would not go to the old men's house, came here. John Quinn came. Before he began his entrance into the old men's house, which we have described, he spoke here with 'weight'. He gambled willingly enough, but he showed himself more and more impatient with the 'playboys' of young fellows. Another man, O'Sullivan, a herdsman of sixty-five and the local 'vet', also came. The rest were younger men, farmer's sons.

But this was a very unstable group. When finally John Quinn moved onward it fell to pieces, and Oscair's hearth was left untenanted each night.

For what shows itself here is a transitional state; the members of the group were in some way or another a little off the centres of their kind in Rynamona. For a moment were gathered here those who could move upward, like John Quinn. Gradually, they could attain full status, they could move into the social place which centres family headship, the land, a line of descent, and the old man's role within the community. Oscair's hearth for them was a roadside resting-place.

With these intermediates were gathered the representatives of another anomalous social place. Both Oscair and O'Sullivan 'the vet' were important figures in the community; their occupations and their skills won them respect and admiration over the countryside. At least, O'Sullivan, the older man, was free to come and go wherever he might wish. But both were 'landless' men; they could never attain full peasant status. In the identifications of Irish familism they were condemned to celibacy; neither could feel comfortable in the old men's *cuaird*. There was no place there for them, except as Oscair's behaviour showed, as 'playboys' and entertainers. So they, too, must occupy an interstice in the structural alignments of rural social life.

For once again the examination of rural life leads one perforce to concepts of structural balance. The organization of the community takes its form in the social behaviour of cliques among the country-people. That behaviour cannot be disassociated from the characteristic alignment of sentiment and interests which at once separates and reintegrates the generations. And the alignment itself in its turn relates the countrymen to one another in the community, upon the basis of relative age, with the familistic nexus in which are balanced prestige, command, the land and the continuities of descent. That to which the countryman is attached is a social order, as Sir Horace Plunkett alone among the commentators on the Irish scene could see. And a social order is an active living growth whose embrace soon gathers in the whole of life.

V

Shops, Pubs, and Fairs

In many ways the town is an alien world, even a hostile one, to the countryman. He feels its scorn of his rusticity and distrusts its urbane way. Yet the town has an attraction for him no less strong in rural Ireland than elsewhere in the world. It weans away his sons and daughters. It brings him the breath of the outer world. After all, metropolis is a relative term. Metropolitan prestige is an infinite gradation in which the smallest hamlet may have a share with Megalopolis. Metropolitan prejudice is no less capable of minute division, and country towns engender little cockneys as quickly as might London produce a great one. They, too, would feel with Dr. Johnson that the fairest prospect in all Scotland was the road to London Town.

For if Megalopolis is the crossroads of the world, the country town is no less so. The difference is merely one of scale. Broadway, Piccadilly, and the Place de l'Opéra have counterparts in any country town.

In Ireland the parallel is more apt than one might credit at first thought. Irish towns have always been little more than crossroad centres. They are market-towns and administrative seats. Their economics is that of distribution, not production. The industrial revolution has passed southern Ireland by. The shop, the pub, the fair bring the towns their life-blood and link them to their hinterlands and to the outside

world. Many of them still collect market tolls on rural
produce, as if they still had a ring of stone-wall fortifi-
cation about them. Many of them have no fair green
but throw open all their streets to shouting, bargaining
men and milling cattle, on the day of the fair, sur-
rendering themselves entirely to the countryside upon
which they live.

One still approaches many of them today as one
approached them in the sixteenth century, although
now perhaps an automobile road breaks a new entrance into them or the railroad halts a jaunting car's
distance away. The roads that radiate inward toward
the heart of the town are still lined with labourers' and
artisans' thatched cottages long before one reaches the
town itself. As one proceeds along them, the cottages
give way to shops and public houses which rise higher
and more stately as one nears the centre, in the
market-place or in the central square. There, quite
often, that emporium of the most valuable commodity
of all—the local bank—now dominates the scene.

Between the shop-fronts, back lanes lead off to the
recesses in which the labourers live; and, off by themselves in a proud segregation, stand the more preten-
tious houses of a residential area, and the great grey
buildings in which local government and justice are
housed. But the centre remains the point at which the
shop-lined streets that lead from deep within the
countryside converge. The life of the country and that
of the town meet and mingle along these converging
lines.

That mingling represents the latest stage of an age-
old struggle in which the countryside has won out at
last. It has been a conquest of assimilation, like the
victories of Chinese life over the barbarian invader.
The town in Irish history was originally, and often
long remained, a foreign growth. In the great age of

Celtic civilization, the monastery and the royal seat centred Irish life. Later the Celto-Norman castle scorned an urban fortress wall. The town was first a Danish importation; only Galway, of Irish cities, was not a Norseman's settlement. Throughout the long wars and counterwars with the English foe and the alien English life, the town was many times alternately absorbed by native life and reconquered for the alien. Even Galway still bore its famous inscription above its city gate not three centuries ago. "O Lord," it read, "deliver us from the fury of the O'Flaherties." Law, at first, forbade even the entrance of the 'Irishry' into the towns and then later decreed that no Irishman should trade with another. The towns were to remain English, and later, Protestant, and the merchant-burghers who flourished in them must remain of English blood and habit.

All that, of course, has long since vanished. The Irish have occupied the towns of their own land, their blood and habit hold sway and fashion urban commerce in the towns and cities. The change has been a slow and durable growth, flowing on beneath the surface of political and cultural strife. But like all growth it has been a process of incorporation, too. Today, to a casual eye, the shops, the commerce, the social life of the Irish town is much like that of all modern western Europe.

Such is the history, briefly put, which has provided the scene that interests the social anthropologist. It is in this scene that he can inquire into the bonds this conquest has created. He can appraise through them the factors which make up the countryman's participation in the larger world. Many fields for investigation present themselves in this connection. Townsmen and countrymen are now equally part, each in his own way, of that whole we name Irish society. From his own vantage each acts toward the other and builds up a relationship with him in such a way as to determine in some degree the form of that whole. This relation, an instance of the age-old reciprocity between town and country, invites our examination.

In Ireland today, one can see this relation most definitely and most significantly in the ties between shopkeeper and countryman. In the west and south of the Free State, at least, the landlord is gone and the true big farmer is rare. The town's hinterland is the world of the small farmers. And the town lives by its connection with the social order to which the coun tryman is attached. One need probe only a little way beneath the surface of conventionalities to learn that the connection is much more than the economics of distribution and exchange.

In the first place, the shop is also the seat of a familistic identification, very like that of land and farm. Ireland is better supplied with shops, at least in number, than any comparable European nation. A very large proportion of her population lives by retail trade. But one must not think of these shops, so numerous in every Irish town, as great department stores, or as units in a country-wide chain. The former, of course, do exist in cities, and the latter, called multiple-shops, are a new invasion. They have little place as yet in the smaller towns. The typical shop is a less imposing affair. It supports, normally, only the family which works it.

Such a shop is most often a small two-story building. The ground floor is evenly divided between the business premises and the household kitchen. In front, a single step in from the street, a single deep room, whose width is that of the building's front, houses counter, shelves, shop-stock and money-till. The business of a lifetime goes forward in this room. In back, a

flagstone-floored kitchen with an open hearth dupli-
cates, on a more elaborate scale perhaps, the country
farm house kitchen. Like its country counterpart it is
the seat of family life.

Upstairs, a front room facing the street is transformed, by family portraits, an ornamental mantle and
a piece or two of good mahogany, into a ceremonial
parlour. Behind this, range the bedrooms of the family. Perhaps, in affluence and refinement there is an
upstairs sitting-room as well. For the shop is no mere
place of business. It is first of all a household, of which
one section and one only is devoted to the world of
affairs.

The family which this household houses and supports, in the majority of cases, works the shop in much
the same way that the family of the farmer works the
land. It conducts its business as a united corporation
in which all members may take a hand and each have
his place. Husband and wife tend the counter together and between them shopkeeping is divided;
sons and daughters work as shop-assistants, as long as
they remain at home. Only when affluence lifts the
shop to importance and dignifies the shopkeeper with
the title and station of merchant, expanding his
business to wholesaling, is this arrangement greatly
modified.

Yet, self-sufficient as this familistic shop-world is,
the countryman has many a connection with it. It
lives its own quiet life and plies its own trade so different from the farmer's work upon the farm. Town
life breeds its own sentiment and weaves its own
bonds, making of the townsmen a community of conduct, feeling and values. But, nevertheless, despite
this isolating process which shuts the countryman out,
he is not at all remote. The first great tie, and the ob-
vious one, is the economic. The country-dwellers buy

the shop goods which move across the townsmen's counters and bring in the moneys realized in fair and market in exchange for retail goods.

But the economic tie is not sufficient, in Irish life, for permanence. Time and assimilation have woven a full social pattern round it. The pattern is really an extension townwards of the countryman's own social order. The market town fills its role as a metropolis of native sentiment in that extension.

There is a saying in the towns of Ireland that summarizes well the movements of town life. "The country-people flock into the towns," they say, "and the townspeople all die out of them." A moment's investigation bears out the fact. Though the town, too, is a familistic world, like the countryside, it differs in that it is a world in slow movement. Generation after generation, a new family sets up shop or public-house, flourishes or fails and then passes on out of the town's life; pressed from behind by the vigour of new country blood or graduated upward economically and socially into the professions. Some families withstand the movement a long time; here and there one can point to a century or more of burgher succession. Others have known a more rapid change of station downward or upward in a single generation. But all of them together can feel the compelling sweep of movement which is part of town life.

Is it really the countryman's vigour that sweeps thus through the Irish towns? I know that is the usual explanation, where such a situation in town and urban life exists. Much has been written in Ireland and in all modern countries about the debilitating effect of urban and near-urban life. It is the fashion to lament the onward sweep which fills the towns and cities with fresh blood, names and faces and pushes out the old. Landmarks change out of recognition; the old families disappear mysteriously, and one can cry out that a new barbarian flood is sweeping away the life's blood of the educated urban classes.

But such a view is very blind. It is astigmatic from a too close looking upon the immediate, instant case. It neglects entirely the organization of human behaviour and sentiment, unreasoned and unplanned though it be, that makes our human societies. It confounds the force of ordered change with weakness and decay.

Nowhere would the view fail worse than in southern Ireland. The countryman who presses in upon the townsman does not drive him out through superior vigour, nor does the townsman fade away in weak decay. Each is caught in a social pattern which fashions many lifetimes and their desires, ambitions, achievements and failures. History and habit have wrought a series of pathways almost as definite as those of a termite's nest; but history and habit care little which termite follows them. Vigour, if it exists, can only be measured in the ease with which the path-follower travels along his course, and the change which his passing makes upon it.

I am sure I shall be accused of a thorough-going, even mystical determinism in human affairs. But let us follow the countryman and the towns-dweller and see wherein my heresy is justifiable and wherein we may temper it.

In the communities my colleagues and I came to know, the country customer who brings his trade into the shop does so in response to the ties of kinship and friendliness. He 'goes with' a shopkeeper or publican, most often, as he 'coors' with his country friends. This is not his only incentive but it is his principal one. The social order of which he is a part embraces the town-dwelling shopkeeper; trade follows friendship. Many indeed are the shops which rely almost entirely upon this 'family trade'. Others know it to be the base upon which they must build.

But, we remember, the relation of kinship and friendship is reciprocal. The shopkeeper is bound in his turn to his 'family trade'. He owes obligation to the 'country cousins' who buy from him. In this way, a durable bond is created which exists over and above the economics of retail trade. It is of the kind that the countryman understands best; it charges the relationship with interest for him; it infuses it with sentiment, habit and reciprocal force. The shopkeeper, too, can rely upon it. Even though he be caught in the demands it makes upon him, he, nevertheless, can rely heavily upon its expectancies.

The ordinary modest retail shop or pub lives upon this tie. In many cases the tie infuses business with a social content which becomes co-extensive with the distributive function the shop performs in economic exchange. If the tie is weakened, if it dies, the shop weakens and dies too. And with it dies the family which derives livelihood, status and much of its corporate existence from that shop. For possession of the shop gives status and prestige and marks one's social place for the family, as much as does the 'farm of land' in the countryside. The family's 'name is on the shop' in much the same way as the country family's name is 'on the land'. In fact, almost symbolically, that name is literally on the shop, for in Ireland most often a single word—the family name—rather than any announcement of the type of retail trade carried on—hangs over the door to proclaim the shop's existence to the buying public. And when the 'family trade' dies, that name dies out of the shop world with it.

Business, then, in the market-towns is no frantic search for better qualities at lower prices. It is first of all a technique in social relations. It demands an orientation to a social order, that of the countryman-customer. Customer and retailer are brought together, not primarily through a cheap price nor an eye-compelling package, but through personalities and through blood and marriage bonds.

In this social context, the interests of shopkeeper and farmer coincide. If the shop is to live it must re-new its ties with the rural hinterland; if the farm on the land is to grow in status and strength it must ally itself in a higher and wider social sphere, and in so doing, provide well for its dispersed children. This coincidence of interest determines much of the shop-keeper's life; through it the countryman has assimi-lated the town to his own way of life.

The town represents that higher and wider sphere for the countryman. Its life is that of a higher station in life; it is a centre of metropolitan prestige. So the farmer can come to send his son into a shop, as he sends a daughter 'into the land' in match-making, to provide him with a better place in life, to make a gentleman of him. The shopkeeper may need a young and pliable assistant in his business. He must have one upon whose kindred he can depend for extension of his trade. He takes in the farmer's son.

In this way, the first of the social bonds that unite the shop and the pub to the rural hinterland is created. A pathway is created along which human lives can move and play out their roles in social life. One of the farmer's sons can hope, with luck and affluence, to become a shop-assistant in the market-town. The por-tion he receives upon the dispersal of the farm family may well take the form of such a start in life. The farmer-father pays the boy's apprentice bond.

Formal apprenticeships still flourish in Irish country towns and nowhere better than in the shop or pub.

The country boy is bound in custom and in law to his new employer and learns the alien way of business and social habit under a master's eye. Eventually he may succeed to a shop of his own, but first he 'must serve his time'. In this, rural Ireland has preserved an older form and charged it with its own peculiar content. The town-bred lad is seldom hired; he brings no rural kindred with him. Then, too, he is neither so impressionable nor so easy to control. The country lad, at first, is both. The shopkeeper taps the social order of the countryside in the person of his fledgling 'prentice boy.

But time brings ordered change in social life, in the town no less than in the countryside. The boy grows up; he serves his time. He acquires the experience and the technique which fit him for the role for which his parents paid his apprentice bond. Unless he is to retain a subordinate and unimportant place as shop-assistant for a lifetime, he must move on. He must acquire a shop himself. And so he does, if he humanly can, and to that end his savings go.

So much for the farmer's son. In his person, he represents a rough one-half of the countryside's invasion of the town. Yet he has sisters, too, at home upon the farm. The attraction of metropolis is no less great for them; they, too, must be provided for in the dispersal of the family upon the land. And with them goes the rural social order and the ties of kinship and community.

In this fact one can see another rough half of the rural tide that sweeps into the ranks of business in the towns. The shop-world taps its country hinterland again in the persons of the daughters of the farms. The farmer must, if he can, marry his daughter off well; prestige and alliance go with her and the dowry which she carries as her portion. The shopkeeper must renew his ties with the countryside with each new generation, if the shop is to survive. In this coincidence of interest, again, a great deal of the marriage custom of the town revolves. The world of shops and pubs is caught within the ordered mechanism of change called *match-making*, in the same way as is the 'farm of land'.

Currently in country towns, the 'match' is the accepted type of marriage for publican and shopkeeper as much as it is for the farmer. The more sophisticated and more affluent shopkeepers, those who are close, or would like to be, to the higher status of merchant, would repudiate the rustic word. They would tell you that they make instead 'proper marriage settlements'. But their humbler fellow-tradesmen, whose shops have not such pretensions, are closer to the soil. They would admit what is for both of them the fact.

Consequently, one can find in the town, round the shop and pub, the same reorganization of human relationships that goes forward when the country match transfers land and household command to a marrying son. But there is one great difference. In the town one must bring a country-woman in.

If one analyses the census of marriage, age and occupation in the Free State made in 1926, one can see how general this reorganization is. It lies behind the statistics of a great part of the country. Without it, one cannot explain the striking uniformity that gives a roughly similar grouping of individuals by age, by sex, by marital conditions, in all the towns, except the large cities, of southern Ireland. For instance, shop-assistants everywhere are young unmarried men and women. Entrance into the ownership of shop and public-house takes place at the same age as does entrance into married state. Though the towns show no such marked extremes as do the country districts, mar-

riage is long delayed and bachelorhood and spinster-
hood are very frequent by world standards. One need
not be a demographer or statistician to be struck with
the parallel, and to wonder at such coincidence between the lives of the followers of occupations so dis-
similar as agriculture and retail commerce.

For this statistical correspondence overlies the facts
of social life. It merely expresses numerically the community of custom between country and town. If one
cares to probe deeper, among the lives whose events
the census records, one finds the custom at the root of
human behaviour and human sentiment. One lays bare
the outline of the balance in which the lives of townsmen and countrymen co-mingle in a larger whole.

For setting up a shop means setting up a family; it
means marriage and the bringing-in of a country girl.
There are exceptions, of course; custom is only a general imperative. Nevertheless, the country match is
the generality.

Most often, the shopkeeper-father turns over the
shop to the son who is to succeed him when that son
marries. The daughter-in-law is the daughter of a
farmer of the countryside. Her people 'walk the shop'
as they would 'walk the land' in a country match. Long
negotiation equates the dowry they give with the
shop, its stock, its debts and its prospects. The two
families cast the agreement into proper legal form.
The shopkeeper transfers his control and his ownership to the son and the son's wife. The other shop
children are dispersed and are provided for, where
possible. The older generation retires; and a new family is established in business in the town.

This is a smooth and orderly transition. The shop
keeps its identification with human ties unbroken,
from parents to children. It renews them once again,
outward into the rural hinterland, in the persons of

kindred the young wife brings 'into the shop'. The shop's life blood is renewed: literally, in the persons of the new master and mistress; socially, in the extensions of kinship and alliance; and economically, because trade follows personal ties.

The erstwhile apprentice boy, the farmer's son, who sets up 'on his own', follows the same course and makes a comparable transition. His marriage and his setting up his own shop most often coincide. His savings and the bride's fortune make possible, together, many a start in the life of the market-towns. Money buys the shop, credit may stock its shelves, but it is the social alliance, contracted in a country marriage, which supplies the trade upon which business rests.

One might ask here if the role of the sexes is not reversible. Might not the young man marry-in into the shop, and the girl rise from assistantship to full-fledged ownership? Naturally, such a course might well be taken; a social order allows many channels. It has not the rigidity of formal law. Or the girl may inherit a shop, or receive one, in the towns, as her particular portion. For to set up a daughter in a small shop is to provide well for her and to assure her station for her lifetime; even though little wealth will come to her through that shop door. But in the scheme of social emphases, these courses are the exceptions. Practically, for a finally successful adaptation, the man must rise through an economic apprenticeship. His is the bread-winning role in social life. Only the bride regularly marries into her new station.

We are dealing here with a social form of nearly universal occurrence where a society preserves some trace of patriarchal form. It is a structural necessity where class lines cross-cut a familistic order. In India, for instance, it is immediately recognizable to the sociologist; for Hindu society incorporates into religious or formal law much of the social custom which other civilizations allow to flow on unheeded, unrecognized and unplanned. There, a lower caste often marries its daughters into the ranks of the next immediately above. The practice is known as hypergamy.

In Western Europe hypergamy is present, in some times and places notably so. The French have recognized it realistically. And here in rural Ireland, the countryman practises it, when he can, though he would be much surprised to hear his efforts on behalf of his daughter so pedantically described. Yet even though the name would mystify him, he would understand the substance of the custom. His daughter is to be married in such a way as to bring credit and alliance to the paternal line upon the farm. That line stands to gain a foothold in the world of shops. For that, the countryman is willing, currently, to pay about twice the usual dowry-price.

And in his willing adherence to custom, stability is achieved. The relationship between class and class, like that in the countryside between kindred and kindred, attains some permanence of form. The bride carries social bonds with her; in this case she carries them upward and townward into the shops and pubs of metropolis.

Her brother, on the other hand, carries with him another social function, in his capacity of male. His place is that of a potential fatherhood in a line of patrilineal descent. He carries on a corporate name upon the land or shop. Where he cannot inherit, in such descent, a sure place among his fellows, he must win it. The man is the bread-winner who carves out a place for his line; round him the family must be grouped. The woman, on the other hand, is the uniting force within the grouping. In this dichotomization of social role between the sexes, the Irish town and the

Irish countryside, like the Church to which they both subscribe, are agreed. Hypergamy takes its form in the agreement. Along the lines laid down by the social bonds of apprenticeship and hypergamous marriage, the world of the market-town and the rural hinterland are united; along the same lines the flow of the country-people townward moves.

Once again, then, we see how complete the inclusions of a familistic order are. The shop lives on and renews its strength. Its owner, whether he be townsman bred or migrant country lad, must 'bring a country girl into the shop'. Marriage, the establishment of a clientele, and the attainment of full status in one's class, all converge at a single point.

This order, one must not forget, is nothing esoteric; it is no more mysterious in the towns than it is in the countryside. Habit, sentiment and desire among the constituent human beings, both make it up and are made up by it. It is really the pattern into which all these melt to make a coherency of social life. Nowhere is this fact better illustrated than in the attitudes the Irish townsmen hold about their own positions within this inclusive pattern. For example, I give you the statement of one townsman, of shopkeeper rank, who could summarize the matrimonial aspirations of his fellows in terms of likes and desires. To us he may seem very conservative and early Victorian in his standards; but he is none the less aware of the demands life makes upon his kind:

"When a shopkeeper marries he wants to get a wife who can help him in the shop. He doesn't want one who has grand ideas about what a fine lady she is, because she is no good in the house and will only drive the customers away. That is why he goes to the country to find a wife. The country girl has been reared alongside her mother, she knows how to cook, sew, keep house, and she hasn't a lot of grand ideas in her head that the town girls have. When she comes to town, she feels she's got on in the world; while the town girl will only be wanting more than her husband can give her, or she won't do her share."

The speaker was a townsman, born and bred, but one can see that he endorsed the system heartily. He was an older man who had made his adaptations to social life successfully.

For others, for those whom the life of the town has caught up and who have acquired 'grand ideas', as the last speaker called them, adaptation is more difficult. The town, as I have said, engenders its own near-urban values. These come to conflict with those which unite the shop world to its countryside. Thus ambition is born, which means a severance of old ties. The ties become thwarting chains, and here and there a young man, caught within the pulls of two incompatible forces, becomes a bitter and scornful rebel.

One such young man, who found himself swept back into the ways of the market-towns after a brief flight into larger horizons in Dublin, fought against the fate that closed him in. He tells his own story: "This town is very dull. I don't understand what brings you here. The trouble with everybody here is that they are all misfits and that they are all in jobs they loathe. Successful men give you good counsel: they tell you to work hard and forget your troubles. But that is because they are in occupations which they like. There is something glamorous about being a solicitor, and everybody comes to you. I would like to have been one. There will be opportunity here when the older men clear out.

"I went off and studied in Dublin for a long while. Then my father died and my mother was stricken with paralysis and I had to come back here and work behind the counter, which I loathe. There's no one else now but my sister. Most shopkeepers make out through their family trade; and the only thing for me to do now is to marry some rich woman in from the country and then all her friends will come in. If you want to get married here there is nothing in it at all but to look out for a country girl. If you don't want to make a fool of yourself and go in for politics, you have to depend on your friends and your wife's friends, and if you can, you've got to marry a girl from the country. Then she'll bring in all her people for miles round, with all their relatives and their married families, and they're the ones that will buy your flour and sugar and tea. You can't get on without them."

In this rebellious young man's lament, another aspect of the life of the towns appears and takes its proper place. The social order which demands the maintenance of personal bonds between countryman and townsman carries with it the seeds of change as well. The young man I have just quoted is caught within the very wheels of this change. A new time and place bring new adaptations in human lives and with them new values which conflict with and destroy the old.

In that fact, simply, lies the explanation of the movement by which the "country-people flock into the towns and the townspeople all die out of them".

The rebellious young man shows well in his own history the point at which change of habit drives the townsman and the countryman apart. After years of near-urban life the townsman loses touch. He can no longer meet the rural ways; he is trained in a different habit; he develops a different turn of mind. He is no longer fitted socially to meet the countryman on the old terms and to respond to the demands the social bonds connecting him with the rural hinterland put upon him. If he is born in the town, a second-generation migrant, he is all the more alien. Metropolis has won his mind, his heart, his soul. New vistas of advancement and new personal ties grow up which attract him further and further into the town's life. The bonds with the countryside are broken; they fall away before a new orientation.

So the shop dies out. The family of which the shop-keeper is a part moves onward. If it is affluent and ambitious, its members rise into the professions perhaps, or seek larger worlds to conquer. If it is not, then oblivion swallows it. It seeks a new place in the ranks of the town in which the countryside has no part. New blood fills its old place along the converging lines of shops and pubs which make up the market-town. The new blood succeeds by virtue of the same ties which originally brought success to the first immigrants from the countryside. It brings with it new bonds of friendship and kinship.

This is a continual movement, a flow along definite pathways in which human lives work out their courses. The country family 'on the land', as we know, buds off with each new generation upon the farm. With the dispersed children go those relationships of a familistic order which unite the human beings in time and space. In this movement ever renewed, yet ever the same, the market-town is caught. Its shops, its pubs, its business life, the whole economic function it performs, flows with this movement.

I have described this relation between the country and the town as though it had no other content than that of kinship bonds. This, of course, is a much too simple view. There are other pathways of success and there are other ties less intimate in nature. But one cannot understand these others till this first has been fully sketched out. For the bonds round kinship and friendship form the great all-pervading base to which all the others must be referred.

In this fact lies a new consideration. In retaining older custom and a more intense emotional and purely social organization of life, Ireland may well have preserved better than most nations of western civilization that unity of spirit which, underneath the surface of superficial strife, welds a nation into a single crucible. If the rationale of economic and social individualism with its attempted divorce between sentiment and logical self-interest seems lacking, the matter is no cause for lamentation or disdain. Who knows ultimately which is the better way? Each people seeks its own better union; unconsciously in social habit, consciously through religion, through politics, through detached and enlightened social thought. Either the conscious or the unconscious may be the more congenial, to nations as well as to individuals.

But danger lies in neglecting one entirely for the other. In the so-called Anglo-Saxon lands one feels that the unconscious organization of social habit has been neglected for the conscious. The logical has been too often mistaken for the ultimate. The all-powerful force of human sentiment has been neglected and too lightly regarded. We are prone to forget, with many an economist, that man not only does not, but cannot and will not, live by bread alone.

The social habit of rural Ireland entertains no such fallacy. In the light of this consideration, the rest of the adaptation of the countryman to his market-town acquires a depth of meaning which lifts it far beyond the plane of the mere economics of the exchange of goods and the distribution of rural and urban products.

For example, a great deal has been said and written about the so-called 'credit system' of rural Ireland. Much indignation has been wasted pro and con upon it. The term refers to the economics of retail distribution in the market-towns. The farmer is often chronically in debt to his shopkeeper. He must live upon credit from fair to fair, paying off a little of his debt from year to year with the price his cattle bring him, but seldom working himself entirely clear. Such a system of chronic indebtedness has analogues in other countries. In Ireland, many commissions have investigated it and many attempts to break its hold have been made. The shopkeeper has been called, sometimes, alas, with cause, a usurer, a 'gombeen-man'. His power as creditor is very great. Where, as here, the farmer-debtor is dependent for his shop-bought foods and farm materials upon the shop, and where no other source of credit exists, that power is, of course, well open to abuse. This is the old problem of equity, the rights of creditor and debtor, and the controls each may put upon the other. It interests us here because in it the countryman's way of life is deeply involved. Let us see what peculiar content his social order gives it.

Any credit system exists, the economist will tell you, upon a peculiar state of mind in which expectancies are roughly balanced. He calls it, sometimes, 'confidence'. Should all the debts be called in and all outstanding obligations mature at a single blow, the system would perforce come to an end. If 'confidence' fails, he will tell you, and a movement to dissolve the fiscal ties grows swift and strong, a crash results. The world has had bitter experience of this fact in recent years.

Yet how little we know even today of that brittle and momentous thing we name 'confidence'! We have the word, but we have not yet decided to what factors it refers. Today we grope toward it in this way and that and wrangle endlessly about the means of creating and restoring it.

In the credit system of the market-towns of rural Ireland, the problem of confidence is a simpler one. Townsmen and countrymen have not yet reached the sophistication of using the word; but they are immediately concerned with the factors to which it refers in their special case. Those factors lie immediately before them, in the social habit which they both follow.

Thus, once the shop has established trade in the creation of the bonds uniting it to the countryside: through the 'family trade' of brothers, fathers, cousins, country wives and country 'prentice boys, that trade must be retained.

The shop must have a permanent expectancy of clientele; the farmer a permanent expectancy of receiving goods and shop articles necessary in the economy by which the farm family lives. The farmer cannot shop about, paying cash; his monetary income comes only periodically: largely in the spring and autumn fairs, to a lesser extent in weekly produce markets. Nor can the shopkeeper depend upon the casual passers-by, for their number is infinitely small. The needs of countryside and town are thus coincident.

In the countryside, I must repeat it once again, kinship and friendship, practically synonymous, provide the base for this coincidence. They make the same provision for the life of the town. They are reciprocal in nature; a favour given is a favour received. A good turn done, the 'friendly thing', creates the expectancy of reciprocity. On such a base a social relationship, reciprocal and permanent, is built.

So the permanence that each party demands is the

permanence of social obligation. The credit system of
the market-towns rests upon this base. In such a situation, the debt the farmer owes, like the fortune he
gives in marriage, is a tangible monetary symbol of
alliance and mutual obligation. To owe money is not
merely to accept a convenience, for either townsman
or countryman. To owe money is to accept a social
obligation.

One can call this disposition the 'confidence' upon
which the credit system of rural Ireland rests. Naturally, the relationship is not perfectly symmetrical.
The shopkeeper, as creditor, has the whip-hand. As
an urbanite, he has the superior status. Yet he is no
less under obligation to his debtor.

Habit and sentiment weave amusing identifications
round this social pattern. For example, to pay off a
debt entirely is perforce to dissolve the relationship.
It is to destroy the mutuality of expectations. If one's
debt is paid off one loses, not only a customer, but a
friend, quite literally. The ordinary small farmer
would pay off all his debt only in a fit of anger. By so
doing he would mean to break the tie completely and
irrevocably. Consequently, he remains upon the shopkeeper's books indefinitely, paying off periodically bit
by bit, but never working himself entirely clear.
Should he do so, the shopkeeper would be fully
warned. He would know his customer was about to
carry his trade elsewhere, and to enter a new tie better suited to his desires.

But the shopkeeper is obligated, too, in his turn. He
may not dun his customer heedlessly. To do so is to
cast doubt upon the customer's ability or willingness,
not to pay a money debt but to meet his obligation.
It is in fact to call into question the social status which
is his. If the shopkeeper errs in this nice tact, the debt

is paid forthwith perhaps, but the relationship is broken.

Nor can he press even a just claim too far. He may often have to carry credit endlessly, in hope of better days. This is part of his obligation, and boycott awaits the offender or the usurper. To carry the claim to court is of no avail; one cannot these days foreclose on land in rural Ireland. Perhaps eventually he might win the farmer's holding from him, in satisfaction of his claim. But one must remember the farmer's 'name is on the land'. A whole kindred and the whole community with which the kindred is related become his bitter and dangerous enemies. In a familistic world that enmity endures for life and longer, even into the next generation.

If even then, in spite of this, the shopkeeper persists and grinds his debtor down, still another sanction closes in upon him. The countryman will make his last resort to age-old folk-belief. He will tell you, for instance, that the shopkeeper or publican dies out because the curses of men and women and the tears and prayers of broken families have wreaked a sure retribution. What better way indeed to express, in traditional mystical and quasi-religious terms, the force of social censure? The countryside can bring its whole traditional scheme of attitudes to bear upon the offender; it can justify the forces of social and personal action in the realm of the awesome mysteries of belief before which all must bow.

Thus one can see why, in folk-belief, money itself is evil. It is one of those mysterious powers which can bring, as though of its own awful and incomprehensible efficacy, both good and evil in its train. The finder of the 'crock of gold' is stricken down in the flush of discovery; the townsman who rises too high and waxes too arrogant in his wealth may soon be stricken, too, and his family and its shop or public-house seems mysteriously to melt away.

Nor is this the only instance in which the social order overlies the economic form of debt and shapes it to its purposes. The debt, like the dowry, can and does become a measure of status, too. It is a sign of one's ability to support that network of social obligation which gives one's self and one's family a place in social life. In this fact, too, lies 'confidence'. The debt descends with the land or the shop from father to son. It moves onward with the progression of the generations. Many a small farmer pays off bit by bit the family debt of a parent or relative. Social obligation, in which pride and sentiment are involved, long outlives the statute of limitations. In this disposition, religion, sentiment and custom coincide. Many a shopkeeper till recently has assisted a boy or girl to emigrate, in the sure knowledge that his or her remittances would eventually reach his money-till.

In the days of the British, a Royal Commission found itself mystified by this so-called 'honesty'. The debt to the landlord, in the form of rent, seemed to them an honest debt. Yet the countryman, often as not, scorned honesty in that direction; though he might bend his last efforts in what seemed to the Commissioners a petty commercial credit system.

They forgot, perhaps, that the landlord was removed from the identifications of sentiment and reciprocity which bound Irishman to Irishman and in which the ties between the countryside and the towns at last are formed. For a favour done is a favour received; and the debt is no more than the monetary sign of a social obligation. The 'confidence' its members have in the rural credit system is their trust in a social order.

What then can one say of that figure of Irish public

life who has contributed so much to humour and story on the one hand, and to the bitterness and cynicism of his opponents on the other? I refer to the shopkeeper or publican in politics. His enemies have a stronger name for him; they call him a saloon-keeper and heap moral coals on his head. His friends, on the other hand, know him as a shrewd and genial soul.

The student of social behaviour and the types it produces cannot and must not join either the moralists or the sentimentalists. He must appraise only for the facts; knowledge is not an ethical judgment, it is the analysis of what is. Those who occupy a social place may be good or bad, brilliant or pitiful; only the place can interest the anthropologist.

This type, the shopkeeper-publican in politics, reached its zenith in Ireland in the years from 1898 to the Sinn Fein times. Only in recent years, since the 1916 Rebellion, have other broad social classes of what used to be called the 'Irishry' made a substantial contribution to organized political life, though all of them figured well enough in patriotic rebellion. 1898 is the crucial date, because then the landlords were displaced in the management of local affairs. The older Grand Jury system, based upon large property qualifications, gave way to the elective County Councils.

At about the same time, land war had broken the last remaining ties between the landlords, as a class, and the social order of the countryside. The growth of the towns since the Famine had by then well established the new relation between the market-town and its rural hinterland which I have described. In the new situation, the shopkeeper and the publican could best represent the united interests of the social order of which they were, in their own way, an important part.

All nations infuse political forms with their own genius. The Irish were not slow to do so; they soon made their own infusion. The reciprocities of a familistic order, in which sentiment and habit found effective organization, were the materials they had at hand. The bonds between town and countryside provided channels through which the infusion could flow.

For, as I have tried to show you, the shopkeeper-publican occupied then, and still does, a strategic place in the organization of the countryside. From that point of vantage he could serve many ends. His business depended upon the social role he performed; the countryman expected favours for favours rendered. He knew best the direct personal approaches of social obligation. So, at first, geese and country produce besieged the new officers and magistrates; a favourable decision or a necessary public work performed was interpreted as a favour given. It demanded a direct and personal return. 'Influence' to the countryman was and is a direct personal relationship, like the friendship of the countryside along which his own life moves. Like money, 'influence' was a somewhat mysterious entity; it seemed to be a powerful agent for both good and evil. But its real content seemed understandable enough; it was an easily recognizable social bond.

Then, too, the shop and the pub was and is the countryman's metropolitan club. The man who worked it was a friend and kinsman, one of one's own kind. Near-urban prestige made him a superior, as one in touch with seats of power, fashion and law. But it made him no more, in the last analysis, than a *primus inter pares*. In all this, the conventional moralistic concept of public administration might well be little developed, on both sides. But there was much popular wisdom.

For the shopkeeper-publican dealt effectively first with the realities in which life, his own and his country constituents', is fashioned. To cry corruption is to mistake the issue. To enforce a political morality without emotional conviction would be false conversion indeed.

Thus, the shopkeeper-publican-politician was a very effective instrument, both for the countryside which used him and for himself. He might perhaps exact buying at his shop in return for the performance of his elective duties, as his enemies charge: but he also saw to it that those duties were performed for the very people who wished to see them done. Through him, as through no other possible channel, Ireland reached political maturity and effective national strength. That strength persists today, despite superficial strife and internal growth and change. And it persists by virtue of its connection with the society from which it springs.

For a social order, we can see clearly now, is a thing of very wide inclusions indeed. The same set of dispositions runs right through, from the 'west room' of remote Luogh to the political life of the market-towns and cities of Ireland. In this study, for instance, we began our examination of the countryman's way of life with a discussion of 'old custom'—folklore and folk-belief. By now it is clear to you, I think, that 'old custom' is more than a dying survival of an age-old habit. It is part of a larger whole, a whole which in its total is co-extensive with the total-pattern of the life of which old custom is still a part. Our two original examples, the 'west room' and 'the old man's curse', which came up in the first lecture, lead one on to an analysis of the countryman's way of life. In its turn, that way of life yields one clue at least to the understanding of a nation and its people.

VI

The Good People

In this last lecture we are finally ready to return to
'old custom'. Folklore is part of the social order which
we have been sketching out. Folk-custom and folk-
belief, even though 'survivals' of an ancient day, have
an important role in the life of the countryman. Something of that role I have already tried to show you.
Ancient belief surrounded and reinforced the conventional division of labour. It gave point and interest to
the necessary changes of social and family life. It
helped provide sanctions and formulae of agreement
in which the local community could pursue and regulate its unconscious organization of human lives. It
cropped up again in the synthesis between the life of
the town and that of the countryside.

What is it then that gives old custom and belief this
power? What does it contain within itself that allows
it to persist and outlive the centuries? The anthropologist Marrett said once: "Survivals are no mere
wreckage of the past, but are likewise symptomatic of
those tendencies of our common nature which have
the best chance of surviving in the long run".

The anthropologist must take note of such 'tendencies' in folklore. Consequently, rather than devote
time to a description of folk-belief as it still exists, I
prefer to attack such questions. In attacking them, I
hope to proceed as we have done before. I shall try to

treat folklore as it occurs in the life of the countryman
and find the answers to our queries there.

In so doing, I must give warning that I must leave
aside a good deal of the most picturesque elements of
Irish folklore. Remnants of hero-tales, fragments of
the sagas of Oisín and Fionn MacCumhaill and the
Fianna are still to be heard sometimes upon the lips
of the old people. A popular history, half-legend, com-
memorates patriots and the enemies they fought, and
weaves itself round the monuments of the past which
crowd the Irish landscape. Norman barons, Celtic
chieftains, noble lines both native and alien throng the
unwritten pages of this history and elbow for room
with saints and martyrs, Cromwellian soldiers, moon-
lighters and 'ripparees', minstrel poets and hedge-
schoolmasters of learning. A great many religious leg-
ends, in fact a whole popular hagiology, still survive,
infusing local piety with romantic glamour. International tales, like those Grimm recorded first in Ger-
many, traceable from India and Siberia to the remotest
Irish coasts, can still be heard, re-garbed in a traditional Gaelic dress. But all these are a popular literature, unwritten perhaps, but none the less evolved in
response to canons of literary expression. They have
been dealt with by more competent commentators
than I.

I must give warning, too, that I am not equipped
to give you the usual collector's report. I can give little
account of the marvellous fauna and flora that filled
the Irish countryside till recently. Better collectors
than I have done ample justice to many a headless
black dog that haunts a road in country districts and
to many a *péist* or *broc-shidhe* that dwells in lake and
cave. Nor can I regale you with the marvellous or
fearsome deeds of 'weasels', 'hares' and 'worms' that
clothe a fairy power in animal form. Likewise the

whole great field of charms and nostrums, magic cures, lucky and unlucky deeds and days and things, is a world of detail into which I cannot lead you very far, except in furtherance of the purpose of this discussion.

For in attempting to relate folklore to social life, interest lies not so much in the minutiae of particular folk-belief as in the part the scheme of thought they make up plays in customary conduct. The problem is not so much just what is believed, but the effect of and the reason for such belief.

In such a discussion, some preliminary definition of the folklore we deal with is necessary. The usual definition is very loose: the unrecorded traditions of the people as they appear in popular fiction, custom and belief, magic and ritual. I prefer rather to narrow the field down, and to leave aside the historical question involved. But even then, we are left with a very broad field of inquiry. All the acts and rituals associated with belief in supernatural powers not directly recognized and regulated by the official doctrine of the Church remain for us to examine.

The chief of these powers is usually called the 'fairies'. The country-people have many other names for them which they prefer. But, most often, they feel no need of distinguishing them by particular names. They call them simply 'them'. In the pronoun they summarize both their nameless power and their immanence. No greater specification is necessary where such powers crowd so closely in upon one's life. The acts and rituals which spring out of this belief are similarly broad in scope. They range from minor doings and turns of speech of daily life to the most hidden practices of rare and deadly black magic.

Perhaps the native name gives the best definition. The whole fairy-cult is under attack these days. The forces of Church and school are pitted against it. It is nothing more than 'pisherogues', the countryman will tell you. The word is usually translated as 'superstition', but the English word contains too great a bias for us to use it. The 'pisherogues' are much more than ignorant superstitions. In the light of an acquaintance with the practices of the world's peoples, they are easily understandable in much broader terms. They form a symbolic order overlying the values of social life and clothing them in emotional terms in much the same way as do unofficial dogmas and unofficial, non-logical cosmologies among all peoples, not excepting those of our own urban civilization of today. In that, they respond to recognizable sociological and psychological necessities. In its own way, Yankee New England is as fertile of such non-logical beliefs as is rural Ireland. Rural Ireland is different only in that she has preserved an older and more ancient terminology in which to build her particular symbolism. She has her own genius in the matter which expresses the age-long continuities of her culture.

I think you will perhaps understand me better if I go on to sketch out the symbolism which the 'pisherogues' contain.

First, one must notice that the Irish countryman is a very devout man. His life is ordered in his adherence to his religion. Much of his habit of mind and his view of the world responds to his Faith. He is a devout and practising Catholic. But he is also devout in another direction too, very often. Just as there is room in his mind and heart for patriotic fervour along with religious zeal, so is there room for fairy belief. Sometimes, of course, these devotions may conflict; but ordinarily they need not. They can intermesh and support one another.

Thus in his daily life, one finds the countryman carrying out many acts which are related both to his

Church and his fairy belief. His allegiance to the first is, of course, definitely greater, but he has room for both. One finds him, for instance, 'blessing' himself on setting out for the day's work, or on beginning a trip or a new undertaking such as the potato-planting, with two purposes in mind. If you ask him, you learn, first, that he dedicates his day or his enterprise to God. He throws himself upon divine protection. Secondly, he seeks that protection to a definite end. He hopes to ward off thus the forces of evil and ill-luck. He hopes to assure himself the enterprise will prosper. He guards himself against molestation from 'the good people'.

That does not mean he is motivated by fear even when 'the good people' are concerned. His devotion springs from deeper and wider emotional sources than mere fear. Rather he makes his peace with the fairies; he pays them their due. His religion is *the* faith to him, and his acts are primarily, first and foremost, acts of religious devotion. But the popular mind is not distressed very much with logical inconsistencies, and somewhere in the act, very secondarily, of course, may lurk the other lesser faith he holds.

Thus, in one aspect, the 'pisherogues' occupy, like nearly all folklore, the border-line between the natural, profane, mundane world and that of the supernatural, the sacred, and the religious. It is along this borderline that we must trace the countryman.

I say fear is not his chief motive. For the good people are not entirely fearsome. I have often heard countrymen, steeped in the old lore, say, "They'll leave you alone if you don't be in their way". One makes a great mistake to think of any holder of popular belief as a person ridden with superstitious fear, unable to make his way through ordinary life. As one countryman told another collector, Lady Gregory, in the days before the war: "If we knew how to be neighbourly with them, they would be neighbourly and friendly with us".

It is a question, then, of giving 'them' their due. Where older custom survives, certain precautions must be taken. You are probably all familiar with many of them. Food and water must be left for them at night. Dirty water must not be thrown out at night. For the night is a 'lonely time'; 'you wouldn't like to be out in it'. The fairies are abroad. Were the water thrown out, there is danger that it might dirty them as they pass along a fairy path or make a nocturnal visit. Then they will be angry, and disaster will follow. A hen, a pig, a cow, even a child may sicken and die.

But this anger of theirs, you see, results from direct affront. And that affront lies, really, in improper conduct. In the case of dirty water, it lies directly in improper conduct of the household. Throwing out dirty water is slovenly and bad management. The community condemns it as much as do the fairies who might be wetted.

Consequently, one can begin to see the existence of a projection of values into the world of belief. Dangerous as 'they' are, they bring good luck and prosperity as well, if they receive their proper due. Their favour follows proper conduct of the household and good household management in daily life. Thus one finds such statements possible as the following, in which an old fellow of North Clare, an authority on such matters, speaks of 'their' nocturnal visits:

"They very often put up at a house in the night. They would come to certain houses, and if they liked the house and it was good and clean and everything swept for them, they would come often to the same house, and that house would be prosperous. If it was dirty and they found no comfort in it they would not stop. They'd go to strong houses like the Careys' [he named a comfortable, neat family of small farmers in the neighbourhood]. You often see a little old woman going along the road and stopping in asking for a bite to eat, and you might give it to her, and she looking to see was it a good house for them to stop in it."

Thus many tales told of the good people point a moral. In this light such a common tale as that of the herdsman's house is readily understandable. The herdsman, as a landless man, is regarded by the small farmers as being a 'cut' below themselves; consequently, his untidiness is a byword among them. One version of the story goes, in synopsis, as follows:

"Many families moved into a herdsman's place, but they were all chased out of it. Finally, one family moved in, cleaned up the house, and a 'paving path' round it. A little old woman visits the wife, borrows a cooking-pot, and is similarly well treated. In gratitude she explains that the woman of the house and her husband will always prosper and never be molested, because they alone of all the families had cleaned up the place where 'they' walk."

In this way the values of daily life are projected into and reinforced by the supernatural world. The same state of affairs holds good even in the convention of social intercourse. The vocabulary of the countryman is full of homely pieties. On entering a house the proper greeting is "God bless all here". On coming upon another at work, one says, "God bless the work". Similarly, "God spare you the health" is 'put on' anyone who 'coors' with you. Any praise of person, child, or animal is accompanied with a "God bless it"; any mention of unpleasantness or danger is followed with some such homily as "God bless the mark", and so on. If one omits such pieties, one is sure to rouse resentment in the listeners. For one must remember that emotion supports these conventions. But the resentment springs from other causes, too. These formulae are known to the folklorist as 'protective formulae'. He means by that that they have reference to the lesser faith as well as to the greater that the countryman holds.

If you ask the countryman why he uses such terms, he will give you several answers. First, "You have right to do it, because you owe it to God", and then, second, "It will bring good luck, it will keep 'them' away". For the countryman, both answers are true. The phrases are both acts of pious invocation and protective devices warding off evil. Their omission is really dangerous. It puts the person or thing so neglected in jeopardy; the negligent speaker is open to suspicion of an evil intent. Thus there are many stories which attribute disease, disaster and death to such omissions. In this way again, persons and things of value to the countryman are brought into the scope of his beliefs and attitudes. The forces which affect them are brought into a shape in which he can understand them and in which he can cope with them.

Perhaps the most interesting part of this process is to be found in the way in which the goods by which the countryman lives are brought into his belief. The good people affect the household and all its goods. They 'take' those things which one values, round which one's interest and sentiments, as a member of the farm-working family, are centred. One Galway woman phrased this idea to Lady Gregory: "They have cows, and sheep, and chickens out in the raths just the way we have them with us. For it is they that take them when the bad luck is on us and then whatever we do won't stop them." The 'other people', as they are also called, are not very different in this regard from ordinary mortals; they surround themselves with much the same materials of life.

So, then, when ill-luck descends upon him, the countryman knows something at least of its nature, enough to allow him to cope with it. Take the example of butter. Butter is an important staple of farm diet; it is of great interest to all the family group. Yet the making of butter, especially with a hand-churn, is a notoriously tricky process. Should it fail to come in the churning, the matter is one of grave concern. One woman of North Clare put the matter very clearly when she said: "And queer things do happen to butter, and it's a fact it often wouldn't come and you don't know why. You'd be trying every way you could and still you'd be without it but for what your friends would give you."

But in that event, the countryman is not left helpless. His belief provides him with a sure knowledge of what the trouble is, and of what may be done about it. The fairies have 'taken' the butter and must be induced to bring it back. Many of the tales he has heard year after year attest to this taking. For instance, here is the synopsis of a story told by a Clare farmer of friends of his, whose house he named:

"Two men return from a fair to the house of one of them to have breakfast. There the woman was churning, but no butter would come. The first of the men suggested maybe they [the men] were holding it up, and they left the house, but with no result, for when they returned there was still no butter. Upon finding out that an old woman, a stranger, had borrowed a bit of milk the day before, the first man closed the doors, took a ploughshare and held it in the turf fire. Soon there came a knock at the door, and after the third knock the woman of the house went to it. Then an old woman's hand passed a jug of milk through the crack of the door and a voice said: 'put this back in the

churn'. She did so, and immediately all the milk
turned to good butter."

But the farmer knows, too, that the fairies do not
always work alone. There is often a human agency
involved along with theirs. Here one enters the
really dangerous 'pisherogues', the practices of wicked
magic. A human being may perform a rite or omit a
precaution in such a way as to bring about a visitation
of ill-luck and disaster. He may transfer disease and
sickness from his own farm to the next, he may steal
the butter of another's churn, he may destroy, steal,
maim and kill by inducing the supernatural powers to
commit the havoc.

But sometimes the human being who brings about
such a visitation upon another does so unintentionally,
innocent of evil intent. A person can be either lucky
or unlucky; he may tap a fairy power without meaning
to. Thus one humorous story, a favourite yarn of the
fairy-lore, found widely over Ireland, relates the mis-
adventures of one rash fellow:

"A man that was usually drunk was going by a fort
one night and he heard 'them' talking in it, and saying, 'I'll take half of it and let you have the other.'
'I'll have all of it', shouted my boy-o, never thinking.
When he got home, his wife was making butter, but
she couldn't get any to come. But now she tried again,
and it came in and filled the churn twice over and ran
over the floor. There was a big farmer near by, and it
was all his butter she was getting. She was an honest
woman and knew the butter wasn't hers and she
wanted to make it known she hadn't anything to do
with it, so she told the priest about it."

Other things than butter are so taken, of course.
Cattle figure prominently in folk belief. Cattle, as we
know, are very important to the countryman. The time
of calving is a crucial event in farm-family life. Con-

sequently, precautions must be taken; danger is abroad, and rites must be performed. If cattle fall sick, other rites drive off the threatening good people and restore the cow to health. Fairy-tales are full of the taking of cattle by the people of the raths.

Thus, cures of cattle and human beings, as well, bring in the fairy-lore. The good people may take anything from hens to men and women. When they mysteriously sap the strength of a man or woman, leaving him or her sick or weak and listless, he or she is little recognizable as the strong helper and friend of former years. The vitality has gone out of him or her. The country-people can believe that 'they' have spirited away the real person and left in his place "some spent old man that they had with them for a long time". The real person is 'away'. Cures, both religious and responding to the fairy-cult, must bring him back. That does not mean that they do not recognize what we might call natural sickness or disease; they do, only too well, from bitter experience. It means only that they have an explanation for it that infuses it with the associations they have about their belief.

For the belief in changelings, about which you all have heard a great deal, has its root in the fairies' 'taking'. In fact, it is sometimes said, as it was to Lady Gregory, that "all persons who die are taken, except the old people". Only for them is death the natural course of events; all others have fallen prematurely into the power of the supernatural forces.

Thus we can see that the countryman's fairy belief is not entirely a catalogue of wonders, by any means. Nearly all the disturbances of his interests and sentiments can be brought into the scope of an emotionally charged explanatory scheme. The trouble overtaking them becomes interpretable for him; he knows what has happened and is in some measure ready to take the necessary steps. The fate of his goods and his fellows affects him vitally, it upsets the attachments he feels. But belief is common property; it is given to him and held for him by that community of his fellows of which he is a part. It is a socially held ideology to which he gives credence and in which he is dependent upon his fellows for ways and means, for corroboration, for solace.

But this ideology is much more than a mere interpretative device. Certain anthropologists have tried to see in magic and magic belief a groping, primitive science; but the concept has failed them if pressed very far. For the fairy faith enforces definite behaviour upon the countryman; it lays down rites and practices which he must perform. If he is to recover his goods that have been taken, restore his threatened animals, friends or children, he must follow a definite course. That course is laid down for him again by his community of belief and habit.

If we examine the course he must adopt to combat ill-luck and disaster, we see a new incorporation into belief of the things he values. In cures, nostrums, and other means of combating evil, the goods upon which he and his fellows are dependent and to which they are attached are once more brought into the scope of belief. They become repositories of 'power'. They come to carry in their own substance the same supernatural efficacy for good or evil which belongs to the good people.

So, when the good people strike, the countryman who still follows the old folklore is not unprepared. If butter fails to come, for instance, he can take a hearth-coal and sear the bottom of the churn. He can apply iron in a variety of forms; for "there is great power in iron". He can use a hazel-stick, of the kind used in driving cattle, to cure cattle, or to give relief from sickness. He can ward off the disease that has struck his farm or household by transferring the dead thing to another's land, thus forcing the evil 'penalty' to follow it. Or, even more simply, he can merely transfer an egg, a potato, the hearth ashes, of his own threatened household to another's land or garden, and the danger goes with them. These practices drive off the 'good people'.

Similarly, when any of the household goods fall into another's possession, there is danger ahead for the household whose integrity is so broken. If butter fails, borrowed hearth-coals, or tools, or milk may hold the cause. One has merely to find the missing bit of goods, restore it to its rightful place, and thus restore the breach through which the good people have made their dangerous entrance into the life of one's family group and its possessions.

Naturally, then, transfer of this sort is dangerous to the persons to whose land the object is transferred. Consequently, the fearsome 'pisherogues' of black magic often take this form. An egg, a potato, a wand of hazel or thorn mysteriously found in one's own garden is evidence of witchcraft, and danger for one's land and stock and family. That the reason ascribed to the outbreak of ill-luck may be arrived at after the fact, makes it none the less compelling. Belief is a social habit which events confirm.

I shall give you two examples, one of them about a dead thing, and another where simple, homely household objects come to have supernatural power. The first is the account a shopkeeper in a country town gave of a countryman-customer of his. "A countryman came into the shop one day and I asked him how things were going. Bad, said he, he was after losing three cows. I asked how was that, and Martin said it was the 'pisherogues'. He was working down in the bog and found the carcass of a cow there. What did you do with it? I asked him. He left it there, said himself. He was not going to move it for fear of the 'pisherogues'. Didn't they carry it there to put the curse on him, and wasn't it the next week his own cows sickened and died? . . . Then I was asking him, why didn't you get a vet, man? Sure, he said, why should I throw good money after a vet, and I knowing very well what happened to them?"

The second example is an account of disaster and its happy termination from a farmer who told the story in a traditional vein, but whose own record of actuality it is. I might say that the role of the curate in the episode was probably very different from that which the countryman imagined it to be.

"A fellow he knows was hilling potatoes and he got three young fellows to help him. Each of them found an egg in the garden, one a hen's egg, the second a goose egg, the third a turkey's egg. [He told this with great dramatic effect.] Well, the man hadn't any poultry on his farm at all.

"The boys went home and told their mothers, and the women told other women about it till it got all round the parish. The curate heard of it and one day he went over to the farmer and stopped in. They talked about all sorts of other things, and finally the curate said, I am sorry for you. Why? said himself. Because you are going to have bad luck. And he told him about the eggs.

"Well, the farmer had terrible hardships. His stock died on him, he'd go out in the morning and find his ewes dead on their backs with their legs in the air and lambs dropped dead out of their wombs. He had five cows in calf and after that spring he had only one cow left. A pig died on him, and his sister took sick, like to die herself she was. [After a time] the curate came . . . and he held masses in the farmer's house.

"He's doing well again now and has a fine lot of stock. That was about four years ago."

Here then one can see a new kind of incorporation of the values of the countryman's life into belief. The goods round which his interests are centred come to be either beneficial or dangerous to the group to which he belongs, depending upon their connection with it in the critical situations which threaten disease and disaster. Ordinarily, there is nothing supernatural or dangerous about an egg or a hazel-stick, to the countryman. But in these special situations, in which tradition comes to his rescue, they take on a wholly different character. Thus we have the seemingly paradoxical case that the things of greatest 'power' are not by any means always the wondrous, unusual, and fearsome things, but the homely articles of use and familiar associations. Iron cures, but iron is not mysterious. An egg becomes a sign of witchcraft; a pinch of salt protects one against evil; but neither are fearsome things in themselves. Yet in critical circumstances they have the power to heal, to hurt, to cure, to destroy.

For what the countryman's belief is doing for him is something belief always seems destined to do, wherever it is found. Tradition is bearing upon him to keep alive and organize the regard his group must feel for the codes of conduct and the objects of use by which it lives. Belief focuses his attention and his emotions upon them. It gives sanctity to his conventions, his needs, and his goods. It infuses them with emotional associations far beyond their normal capacity to carry sentiment. It gives them symbolic form.

In this way it holds before him, in emotion, in ritual act, in hope of cure, and defence against evil, the important place they have in the social life upon which he is dependent in habit and sentiment. It throws him back upon the secure and stable order of ordinary, traditional life.

In this fact lies the strength of folk-belief. But you may ask, how can this be? How does a belief in the curative powers of an object both throw him back upon his social habit in such a way as to secure him emotionally in it, and effect the purpose of the cure?

The answer lies in the part established association plays in psychological balance. The cures restore; they provide a form of action in which the countryman can regain an emotional equilibrium. The hazel-stick is his sure and habitual means of driving cattle; the egg is his tried staple of diet; iron is his old friend in tools and implements. They all figure in his own habit and in that of his group's life; they are all tried and true associations of his normal security. He sees them as more than mere unrelated things; he sees them as vital parts of his normal security.

Then, when disease and death stalk his possessions and his friends, and threaten him in his regard for them, the countryman makes his appeal to the tried and true. If a cow is sick, he may well try castor-oil first, for he is a rational man. But if castor-oil is unavailing, then other means can be tried. He seizes upon a symbol of normal associations and habitual undisturbed security. The means he adopts restores not the cow so much as it does the peace of mind of him who uses it.

And the belief he holds makes a logical synthesis between this act and the cause of his disturbance. It fits them both into a symbolic order above and beyond, yet closely bound up with, the order of his own life. Put into words, this synthesis takes causal form. "There is great power in a hazel-stick", he says. "It drives 'them' away." And the statement is perfectly true, in the logic of emotions.

In some such way as this, ever broader areas of his associations with normal social life are given 'power'. They are incorporated into belief and wield the same forces of restoring and upsetting that life as do the good people, whose attributes they become. Events, personalities, landmarks, are brought into this order, in one way or another. Nearly everything here below comes to be projected, in imagination traditionally refurbished, into the other world of awe and wonder and mysterious 'power'. The countryman relates himself to the things so projected through their place in his belief; he knows what to do about them and finds his regard for them fashioned in the common folk faith.

The fairy-belief becomes a world-view, a *Weltanschauung*, in which all experience has a place in the logic of emotional associations. Thus one old fellow summed up a discussion of the sea creatures which still haunt the western coasts of Ireland: "Everything that does be on the land is in the sea, too, if we could see them". This world-view incorporates the world into the life the countryman follows and knows. To the same old fellow, winds along the Clare and Galway border that separates Munster and Connaught provinces could appear as the battles of fairy hosts, for do not men today still remember human battles and still taunt the men of the other province in joke and banter? The rustle of a breeze and the flitting of bats in a ruin where men lived and died is not mere noise; it is still part of human life. One old fellow described to me the experience of 'them' that he got at close quarters, when he lived near the ruin of Ballyvaughan workhouse:

"They were so plentiful there that everybody living

round it and myself got so used to them that we wouldn't mind them at all. The place is full of them and everywhere you go there is a door and long windows in the cowl, and you hear them going in and out. There was a great lot of people died in it long ago in the bad times. They are in every room and you hear them on all sides of you. I got so used to it, I never minded them at all, but I heard them every day."

The great cliffs of Moher on the Clare coast are a landmark notable enough for many a legend, but the tales of it that best survive are those that relate it to the life of the present and express in the fairy-belief its danger to human life and property. "There's somebody lost," I was told, "off every bit of the cliffs. In the old days the men used to go down often [for wood and salvage]. They used to go down on their own ropes. . . . There was a fellow over in Liscannor who would go down at any time of day or night. He used to go down for lost sheep or lambs. One day a child fell off Aillenasearrach and he went down for the body . . . but when he came up he said he'd never go down again because every rock down below was covered with people sitting on it. People out of the sea they were. . . . Two little girls were lost looking for flowers the fairies put there to grow. The flowers aren't there at all, but are put there just to draw people over the cliffs."

Thus belief and rite in folklore conspire to a common end. They provide the countryman with a world-view in which his regard for things and scenes and events is charged with the emotional forces necessary in his social life.

But as we have seen again and again throughout our whole discussion, the sentiments he holds are organized first and foremost round his fellows: the members of his family, household, kindred, and the community. It is toward them that his habit is fashioned and in his relation to them that his social order takes its form. Consequently, we should expect fairy-belief and rite to symbolize the regard he has for his fellows even more strongly than that he holds to the non-human associations of his life.

The expectation is amply borne out. Fairy-belief is first and foremost a symbolism of social life. In the logic of emotional identifications, it organizes, directs, and controls the feelings of human beings for their fellows.

Thus fairy power and dangerous influence are strongest at times when the interest of human beings in their fellows is strongest. With every change over-taking the individual in his course through life among his fellows, the supernatural world steps in. At such times as birth, growing-up, marriage, becoming a parent, growing old and dying, belief catches the countryman in a web of precautions and reminders which signalize forcefully the importance of the change. For example, the birth of a child is not just another event in nature. It is a change of vital importance to the family group, and indirectly to the community. It is cause for rejoicing and congratulation, but it is cause, too, for resolve and determination in the face of new duties. It brings a new orientation in the lives of those who welcome the newcomer. Their relations to one another undergo development; they must henceforth learn new ways which include the newcomer and which prepare a place for him in the life of his fellows.

Consequently, rural ceremony signalizes the event. Custom brings together those concerned, for rejoicing, for recognition of the place of the newcomer in the group, for an expression of the sentiments that unite them all. The rural 'christening' is no mere idle jollification; it is a secular baptism, as important for social life as is the Sacrament of Baptism for religion. Naturally, then, fairy-belief is represented very strongly. It surrounds the crucial event of birth and its consequences with a hundred necessities of action which carry with them powerful emotional dispositions. Fear, awe, wonder, religious feeling, and plain caution can all be pressed into service to mould the countryman into an acceptance of the new state of affairs; the logic of belief fits these emotions into the countryman's world-view.

The good people are particularly active at such times as this. Every association with birth is infused with power and danger. Even the midwife who attends becomes a magic figure; the aura that surrounds the dangerous and crucial event invests her entire personality. She can command the fairies, disperse their attacks, travel through the air, transfer labour pains at will to a truculent or negligent husband. She is in communication with the fairy powers; in tale and story she often finds her ministrations commandeered by them and her person wafted off into the forts and raths to attend a fairy-woman there. She herself may deny all this; but it is true, none the less, in belief. Like all else at birth, she is linked to the good people, and in the linkage an explanation is given for the identity of the emotional associations which surround both her and them.

Similarly, all other crucial changes in social life, as well as those of the religious life, come to fit into the same scheme for many of the country-people who still follow the old tradition. The good people figure in them all.

Thus, First Communion and Confirmation—events of first magnitude in the life of the devout countryman —bring changes in emotional well-being; they bestow a real, if mysterious and holy, strength. This, of course, is first of all a part of religious experience. But the events are also accompanied, in the countryside, by changes in one's relations to one's fellows, in traditional social organization. The child is separated first from others of opposite sex after First Communion; he is introduced to full farm work and, very often, leaves school after Confirmation. His fellows in family and community must henceforward have a new regard for him and treat him differently. So, in these changes, the good people have their role, too. Precautions against their influence reinforce one's dependence upon a symbolic order which incorporates these changes. They make definite and unforgettable the magnitude of the change and the new dispositions which must be learned. Thus, again, emotion is enlisted in the fashioning of social habit.

If we leave aside marriage, where folk-custom and folk-belief are no less important toward the same ends, we can devote our attention to the greatest change of all. Death brings the greatest disturbance in social habit. It shakes emotional equilibrium to its foundation. Yet society must allow for death; it must provide an orderly transition and continuance.

The devout Irishman, of course, finds his greatest consolation in his Catholic Faith. He knows the fate of his loved ones. His religion teaches him how to communicate with them, in the Communion of Saints, through prayer. Faith heals his hurt and it gives him a way of filling the void death creates.

Yet, as I have said, he has room in his heart and mind for the fairy-belief too. Social life must take account of death no less than religion. When death removes one of the human beings to whom he is related as brother, friend or fellow, it leaves behind the traces of sentiment and habit that were once bonds of relationship and association. These must be reformed, and in the reformation a new synthesis between the dead member of the group and the living be found. The countryman resembles us all in this respect; he cannot forget 'the old familiar faces'. He must have an explanation in the world-view of folklore and folk-custom for the effect they still exert upon him after they are gone.

So the dead join 'them'. On the border-line between the mundane world and the mysteries of Faith, they find a place in the ranks of the good people, as the misnamed fairies are often called. They are the denizens of rath and fort and hill and cave. There is nothing fundamentally incompatible between this and religious belief, however folklore may escape the control of dogma and sometimes, in its humbler vein, run counter to it. The dead do affect the living, in memory and in tradition. Death is the 'other world' to which we are all advancing. As one fellow could say in a burst of poetic imagery growing out of folk-belief: "The old people in the west room are going down with the sun".

Why not indeed, when we remember that the good people are not always by any means evil and forbidding? They exert their power for both good and evil. They bring reward as well as punishment. The countryman has friends among them as he has friends among men in this world. An Aran woman put the belief for Lady Gregory in words which transport earthly loyalties to the other world. "There's often fighting heard about the house when one is sick. That is what we call the fighting of friends, for we believe it is the friends and enemies of the sick person fighting for him."

Indeed, the same aids that make up habit and give base to sentiment in mundane affairs can be projected into the after-world. One must act toward 'them' in death as one acts toward the living; one must do the 'friendly' thing. Thus they can tell a story in Luogh of a man there who they say "was walking along the road and he saw the ghost of his brother. He didn't say anything to it and it walked home with him all in silence. They sat at the fire for a long time, the [living] man waiting for the other to go, so he could go to bed. Finally, the dead man said: 'You have put me to great trouble tonight by not saluting me when we met. I must go now and now I won't be able to defend you in the council in the rath.' And it was true for him, too: the cow that was ailing with the man was taken the next week."

Thus, you see, one can envision 'them' both in mystic terms and in terms sometimes very bald and intimate indeed. The younger people in Luogh still follow the old belief, though they leave its expression to their elders. Yet they could explain the tumour on an old man's head in words which show how near 'the other people' are and how direct is the aid one's friends among them can give:

"Old Seumas was coming along the road drunk and he met a crowd of them on the road and one of them slapped him. If he'd taken the slap he'd be all right but he took off his coat and dared any one of them to stand down to him. They beat him and gave him a terrible knock over the poll. One of them that was great friends with him saved him."

Nor are 'they' always fearsome, even in their most wondrous apparitions. The dead are too much a part of life in rural Ireland for that. For the old people they are too near; too many friends have crossed the line between this world and the next.

Thus the dead may come to cover nearly every association of life; in the eyes of some of the old people, the other world of wonders where the 'other people' reign spreads all about them. To the initiate in such mysteries there is nothing to fear. Let me give you my record of one conversation of mine with a very old man of North Clare, a man of clear mind and great folk-learning. His answers to my naïve questions will show you how well he felt, accepted and expressed the symbolic order of the countryside:

I asked what a 'cowl' was. "They are the houses where the family has died out of them. People would live in them if they wasn't too bad, falling down and dirty. You often see old people sitting in them." "What people?" I asked. "The people that used to be in it," he replied. "Do you mean ghosts?" He answered me scornfully: "You might see lights in the cowl and you going along the road at night and you pass people you don't know and you can't tell if they are ghosts or not. Of all the people you pass in the town, how would you know what it is they are?"

Only the young men, like myself, would be frightened by this uncertainty in rural Ireland. For all but the old people, such mysteries are awesome and compelling. Once again, folk-belief fashions itself for a social end. In belief the believers unconsciously agree upon an emotional organization of human relations; folklore expresses once again the organization of the community upon age and upon the past. The old couple who move in among the fairy influences and the symbols of family tradition and sentiment in the west room, the old people in whom rural kinship is centred and through whom sentiment is directed to the mystic past of ancestral blood lineage, the old men and women round whose influence the local community patterns its local life, need not fear greatly the imagery that symbolizes the very place they occupy. Rather they can come to immerse themselves in it. They grow very learned in this lore. They are the ones who sometimes come to manipulate it. They are themselves, sometimes, half fairy. 'Wise men' and 'wise women' are always old. It is no accident that the commonest representation of the fairy power is an old man or woman. They are the initiates in the mysteries of the fairy faith.

In this fact one can see the final synthesis between social habit and belief. Rural kinship organizes men and women in a common orientation backward and upward toward the dead and the ancestral. The community bestows ever greater status and influence as one progresses further and further toward the age-grade of the old, in whom tradition and precedent are preserved and expressed. In the sphere of credence and emotion the fairy faith acts to the same end and is so designed. The design, in this instance as in all the others, is not conscious; no one has planned it. It is a design drawn from the social order and acting back upon it. Its imagery is traditional, but its efficacy is of the present. And for that reason it lives.

Thus, in the identification between the old, the dead and the influences which affect the goods, the conducts and the values of the countryman's life, the symbolic order is completed. Folk-belief, in the ancient fairy-cult, with its age-old imagery, makes a complete emotional synthesis, overlying and reacting back upon the sentiment and habit out of which it springs again and again with each generation that learns the old way of life. Consequently, each new generation works a change upon it; elements of the synthesis undergo constant re-embellishment and shift of emphasis. Both old and young are controlled by it, but each in a different way. Today the young are sceptical and a little rebellious; they repudiate much of the older imagery. All that the Church condemns in the 'pisherogues', they also condemn. Today folk-belief is undergoing marked change like all else in this world, like all else in Ireland.

But that does not mean the death-knell of folklore, as some students of folklore seem to think. Far from that, it means only that a symbolic order like any growth in human life must change and grow onward. New forms and new imagery will grow up to clothe in emotional terms the necessary reformations of habit and sentiment in social life, and new syntheses will fashion new belief, changing the old or supplanting it inch by inch.

One can see this process at work in rural Ireland today. Those who repudiate the fairies repudiate only the outmoded symbols, the outworn images. They do not deny the necessity of a symbolic order in their own lives. The student of man is coming to think today that they could not do so, because no people can. There must always be some socially efficacious organization of the sentiments of social life in the logic of belief and imagery. Belief provides first of all a conception of life; then, and then only, does it carry on to become a conception of the world. But life among men includes emotional attitudes at once very necessary and very satisfying; one can starve the spirit only so far. And for that reason the logic of a social order is not that of science and prose, it is that of emotion. Consequently, those of the countryside who repudiate the older symbols merely demand that their emphasis be shifted. They do not cry out for bald science, nor abandon symbolism. They merely insist upon new symbols.

There are currently two directions in which the shift can be made. And, as usual, the popular mind has room for both movements; for they are related, and both are compatible with the countryman's social order. The first direction leads more deeply into the greater Faith of the countryman. Religion can come more and more to provide the emotional balances necessary in social life. Thus Catholicism is a growing, spreading force in the countryside, overtaking many an area of the mind where the 'pisherogues' still flourished till recently. The second direction leads to a reaffirmation, in ever stronger form, of that part of belief in which the dead and death are related to the disturbances and the securities of social life. After all, this is one of the indispensable cores of faith, and it expresses most forcefully the organization of life upon tradition and continuities. It can be retained even if the more picturesque imagery must go.

It is for that reason that the fairy gives way more and more to the ghost in rural Ireland today. Dead 'Tans' now patrol the roads where the banshee may have walked. In stressing the part of the dead in folk-belief, the necessary synthesis between emotional associations and social life can still persist and respond to change and growth. The ghost does his work as well as does the fairy, though he is perhaps less given to poetic dress.

In the treatment of death, one can see the social system of rural Ireland in the full perspective of its deep-rooted strength. In the flashes of poetic genius which seem so prone to trip from an Irish tongue, death acquires a deeper and more poignant meaning than many another racial tongue could give it. And so it is in the mundane, prosaic world of social life. The most important secular ceremony of rural life is the wake and funeral. In the crowds that come to the wake-house to pay their respects to the dead and condole with the living; in the long lines of marching figures, traps, jaunting cars and motorcars that make a slow procession over the open roads from wake-house to church and from church to graveside, the observer glimpses an epitome of rural life in which all its values are mingled.

Kinship bonds are at their strongest. Traditional custom enforces upon the kindred important roles in laying out the dead, in carrying the coffin, in digging the grave, in keening him, in reciting funeral laments that are the last survivals of bardic elegies, in preparing entertainment for all comers, in which the dead man's survivors proudly affirm their place and his in the life of the community.

In all this the fairy-lore takes part. The banshee's cry is merely the funeral keen issued from a fairy voice. It signalizes death in the symbolic world just as the keen of the living signalizes living personal loss. It is the lament over common loss in a common cause, for relatives of the dead must greet each other with the keen at the wake-house.

The goods of household and farm suffer incorporation into emotional symbolism once more; precautions must be taken to protect them and prevent their going beyond with the lost one. Time and place of death are clothed with a hundred supernatural associations.

The reciprocities which make up friendship and give status in the community get full play. Every man, in death, can command a multitude. To stay away, to make no recognition of the day, is to give deadly affront. Every 'right Irishman' turns and walks, if only a few steps, along with the procession. In towns, all the blinds upon the street are drawn and shop-fronts are boarded, in recognition. In the Gaelic tongue, indeed, one and the same word does service for both funeral and multitude. And in the fairy-lore "there is never a funeral but the other people are at it, too, walking along behind". Many a countryman, steeped in the old lore, sees in a whirlwind or puff of mist a *socraid sidhe* or fairy-funeral.

He knows thereby that somewhere the chief expression of traditional social life is calling the countrymen together through a whole countryside for a re-enactment, both solemn and gay, of their sentiments about their fellows and about their view of life and death and destiny.

Index

Age status, 63–67, 107–11, 113, 114, 116
  division of labor, 63–66
Anthropologist, 21–25, 27–30
  detachment of, 29
  social anthropologist, 34–35, 105
Anthropology, 21–30, 34–35
  as operational science, 30
  development of, 23–27
  physical anthropology, 34–35
  social anthropology, 26–30, 42
Apprenticeship, 63–64, 144–45, 148
Archaeology, 33–34

Birmingham, George, 33
Black magic, 42, 175–76
Blood, 84–80, 99, 102, 103
  See also Familism; Kinship

Cailleach, 114–15
Carleton, William, 102
Caste, 100

Catholicism, 32–33, 165, 166–67, 182–83, 187, 189
  See also Religion
Cattle, 51–52, 53, 54, 97
  in folk belief, 172–73
Celtic past, 31, 33–34, 138
Census: 1926, 48–50, 95–98, 146
  1936, 98 n
Ceremony, 113–14, 174, 181–83
  birth, 181–82
  match-making, 77
  protective formulae, 169–70
  wake and funeral, 116, 189–91
Childbearing, 90–91
Childlessness, 92, 126
  'country divorce', 92
Child's role, 57, 63 67
Clan, 33, 84
Cliffs of Moher, 36, 180
Cliques. *See Cuaird*
Comhair. See Cooring
Conversation, 30, 117, 122–30
  See also Cuaird

Co-operation, 69–73, 111
  'lending a boy', 70–71
  See also Cooring; Friend-
    liness; Kinship
Cooring, 72–73, 169
  between shopkeeper and
    countryman, 142
  in Rynamona, 122
'Country divorce', 92
'Cowl', 186
Credit system, 155–58
Cuaird, 122–30
  as structural center, 132–
    35
  of old men, 119–20
  of young men, 130
Custom, 30, 38–47, 104,
  147, 162, 163
  age status, 108
  in farm work, 58–59
  local cattle fair, 52
  'new woman', 90–91
  'old man's curse', 42–46
  'west room', 38–42
  See also Tradition

Death, 183–91
  'cowl', 186
  wake and funeral, 116,
    191
  'west room', 39
Debt, 159
Delargy, Mr., 36
Diet, 52, 56–57, 60
  privilege and precedence,
    117
Diffusionist technique, 25–
  26
Division of labor, 61–66

  age, 63–66
  sex, 61–63
Dowry, 78–81, 103
  in town and country
    match, 147–49
  See also Marriage;
    Match-making
Dupertuis, Wesley, 35
Dynamics, 83

Einzelhof, 54
Emigration, 83–86, 95–98,
  144–47
  apprenticeship, 144–45
  town match, 145–47
Equilibrium, 83, 86, 93
Evolution, 23–25

Fairy lore, 31, 102, 144,
  165–91
  as *Weltanschauung*,
    179–80
  defense against fairies,
    174, 177
  in *cuaird*, 130
  wake and funeral, 190–
    91
  'west room', 38–40
  See also Folk belief;
    'Pisherogues'; 'Powers'
Familism, 54, 68–69, 94–
  95, 99, 105–6, 148–49
  of artisans, 102
  of shop, 139–41
  See also Blood ; Kinship
Famine, 95, 97, 99
Farm, 38, 48–55
  small farm, 51–55
  statistics, 49–50

Father-son relationship, 65–67, 112

Field work, 25

Folk belief, 158–59, 178–87
  as *Weltanschauung*, 179–80
  cattle, 172–73
  'cowl', 186

Folklore, 31, 36–46, 61–62, 63, 163–66, 171–75, 188–91
  black magic, 42
  'old man's curse', 42–46
  preservation of, 33–34
  'west room', 38–42
  See also Folk belief; Tradition

Free state government, 34, 48

Friendliness, 72–74, 84–86, 190
  See also Cooring; Kinship; Reciprocity

'Haggard' (farmyard), 55

Harvard University, 34, 35

Harvest, 60, 70–73

Hencken, Hugh, 34

Herskovits, Frances S., 24

Herskovits, M. J., 24

Hooton, Dr., 34, 35

Hospitality, 74

Hypergamy, 149–50

Inheritance, 65, 77, 81, 87, 92–93

Irish Folklore Journal, 36

Kimball, Mr., 35

Kinship, 44–46, 73–75, 84–86, 113, 142–43, 153–54, 187
  credit system, 155–58
  obligations, 74
  security, 75
  wake and funeral, 190
  See also Blood; Familism; Friendliness

Land, 99, 102–3, 105–6
  See also Familism

Language, 36, 37, 73, 114–15, 189

Luogh (community), 36–38

Lynd, Helen M., 29

Lynd, Robert S., 29

MacNamara, Brinsley, 21

Magic, 42–43, 63, 117
  black magic, 42

Malinowski, Bronislaw, 24

Man's role, 56–57, 61–63, 149–50
  See also Roles; Status

Marrett (anthropologist), 163

Marriage, 41, 77–81, 87, 93–94, 96–98, 101, 126, 146–47, 152
  See also Dowry; Hypergamy; Match-making

Match-making, 77–81, 146–47, 152
  See also Dowry; Hypergamy; Marriage

Movius, Hallam, 34

'New woman', 81, 90–91

Non-normative science, 24

Old-age pension, 88

'Old custom'. See Custom

'Old man's curse', 42–46, 74, 162

Old people, 41–42, 46, 87–90, 98, 107–10, 113, 116–18, 186–87
  See also Age status; Cuaird; Kinship

O'Rahilly (eighteenth-century poet), 112, 114

Pareto, Vilfredo, 24, 112

Patriarchy, 63, 65–67, 148–50
  See also Man's role

Physical anthropology, 34–35

'Pisherogues', 166, 172, 175–76, 189

Plunkett, Sir Horace, 85, 135

Politics, 129
  shopkeeper-publican, 160–62

Population statistics, 95–96

'Powers', 174–75, 177–79

Prestige, 68–69, 80–81, 102–3, 107
  See also Status

Primitive behavior, 23–24
  minuscule social system, 27–29

Protective formulae, 169–70

Reciprocity, 62, 111, 138–39, 143–44, 155–59, 190
  tribal, 29
  See also Credit system; Kinship

Recreation, 31, 112, 130–32, 118–20
  See also Cuaird; Hospitality

Relativity, 24

Religion, 32–33, 115–16, 164, 166–67, 169–70, 188–89

Remittance, 86

Roles, 62–66, 110–11, 115–18, 149–50
  privilege and precedence, 116–18, 128
  See also Child's role; Man's role; Status; Woman's role

Rudimentary forms, 27

'Rundale' (type of settlement), 54

Rynamona (North Clare community), 119–35

'Saint', 45, 114–15

St. Bridget's Day, 59

St. Patrick's Day, 59

Seasons, 58–61

Shop, 139–48, 150–53, 155–59
  apprenticeship, 144–45
  credit system, 155–58
  familistic unit, 139–40
  'family trade', 142–44, 156

Shrovetide, 59, 104

Social anthropology, 26–30

Social censure, 45–47, 101, 108, 130, 158

Social order, 162, 188
primitive society, 27–29

Social stratification, 99–101, 103
See also Status

Statistics, 48–50, 95–98, 146

Status, 66–67, 99–100, 116, 122–30, 134, 143, 159
honors of young men, 132
metropolitan prestige, 136 ff.
of artisans, 102–3
of old people, 87–90, 107–11
See also Age status; Blood

Structure, 76, 83, 135

Superstition, 33, 40
See also Fairy lore; Folk belief; 'Pisherogues'

Survivals, 23–24

Symbolic order, 179, 188

Synge, John M., 113

Tír na nÓg, 41, 42

Tobacco, 117–18

Town, 136–38
economics, 136
familism, 141
flux, 141, 152–53
history, 136–38
near-urban values, 151–53
reciprocity with country, 139–48

Tradition, 31, 33–34, 36, 40–41, 57, 63, 106, 112, 117–19, 130, 177–78, 191
in match-making, 77–81

Trobriands of Melanesia, 29

Wake, 116, 189–91

Warner, Mr., 35

'West room', 38–42, 46, 77, 107, 162, 184

Woman's role, 55–58, 61–63, 92–93, 149–50
emotional role, 67

'Writings', 81

American Museum Science Books are a series of paperback books in the life and earth sciences published for The American Museum of Natural History by the Natural History Press, a division of Doubleday & Company, Inc.

*Alland, Alexander, Jr. *Evolution and Human Behavior* B7

*Asimov, Isaac *A Short History of Biology* B6

*Bennett, Wendell and Junius Bird *Andean Culture History* B9

*Bohannan, Paul *Africa and Africans* B8

* Branley, Franklyn M. *Exploration of the Moon* (Rev. ed.) B1

*Bronowski, J. *The Identity of Man* B15

*Curtis, Helena *The Viruses* B14

*Deetz, James *Invitation to Archaeology* B16

Drucker, Philip *Indians of the Northwest Coast* B3

Hartley, W. G. *How to Use a Microscope* B10

*Lanyon, Wesley E. *Biology of Birds* B2

Linton, David *Photographing Nature* B7

Lowie, Robert *Indians of the Plains* B4

*Michelmore, Susan *Sexual Reproduction* B11

Oliver, Douglas *Invitation to Anthropology* B5

*Silvan, James *Raising Laboratory Animals* B13

Wallenquist, Åke *Dictionary of Astronomical Terms* B12

*Also available in a Natural History Press hardcover edition.